STUDIES IN ECONOMICS AND BUSINESS

Books are to

Environmental

Economics

Third edition

David Burningham
Brunel University
and
John Davies
Coleg Harlech, Gwynedd

Series Editor
Susan Grant
Abingdon and Witney College

Heinemann Educational Publishers
Halley Court, Jordan Hill, Oxford OX2 8EJ
Part of Harcourt Education

Heinemann is the registered trademark of
Harcourt Education Limited

First published as *Green Economics* in 1995 in the Studies in the UK Economy Series
Second edition published 1999
Third edition published 2004

08 07 06 05 04 03
10 9 8 7 6 5 4 3 2 1

British Library Cataloguing in Publication Data is available
from the British Library on request.

ISBN 0435 33226 0

Edited by Catherine Matthews
Typeset by Tech Type, Abingdon, Oxon
Printed and bound in Great Britain by Biddles Ltd, *www.biddles.co.uk*

Original illustrations © Harcourt Education Limited, 2003

Illustrated by TechType

Acknowledgements
AQA for questions on pp. 10-13, 50-1, 60 ©AQA examination questions are reproduced by
permission of the Assessment and Qualifications Alliance; the BBC p.91; Cambridge
University Press on p.5; Crown Copyright pp.8, 41, 67, 70, 106, 107 Crown Copyright
material is reproduced under Class Number C01W00141 with the permission of the
Controller of the HMSO and the Queens printer for Scotland; Daily Express p.34; Daily
Post pp.64, 77; Defra pp.6, 48, 109; The Economist Newspaper Limited pp.37-8, 56, 58-
60, 99; pp. 37–8, 101–104 are Edexcel examination questions reproduced by permission of
London Qualifications Ltd, Financial Times pp.24, 101-02;© The Guardian pp.2, 74, 112,
116, 118-19, 121; The Highways Agency p.78; The Independent pp.26-7, 92, 98; pp.26-7,
91-3, 118-19 reproduced with the kind permission of the OCR; Pluto Press Ltd p.76; The
Reader's Digest Association Limited pp.50-1 by permission of the Reader's Digest
Association Limited, Facts at Your Fingertips ©2001; *Storms Brewing* by David
Montgomery and *Sky pollution* by Alistair Dalton ©The Scotsman Publications Limited
pp.10-12; © NI Syndication, London (19 June 2000) p.102; The Western Mail p.44; Welsh
Water and the Water Services Association for the pie chart and extract on p.16.

Every effort has been made to contact copyright holders of material reproduced in this
book. Any omissions will be rectified in subsequent printings if notice is given to the
publishers.

Tel: 01865 888058 www.heinemann.co.uk

Contents

Preface

The environment figures prominently in the A level Economics specifications. It is one of the options in AQA's Module 3 *Markets at Work*, and is a significant part of Edexcel's Module 2 *Markets: Why they Fail*, OCR's Module 2882 *Market Failure and Government Intervention* and Module 2885 *Transport Economics*. The environment is also a popular topic in degree, HND and UCE economics and business studies courses.

David Burningham's and John Davies' book has proved to be a popular title in the SEB series. This third edition has been substantially revised to take into account new information on, for instance, the Environmental Kuznets Curve, and developments in national and world approaches to environmental issues.

Sue Grant
Series Editor

Introduction

'There is a global emergency going on. The Earth is heating up, and everyone's future is at risk. Please join us in sending a strong message to our governments that now is the time for action to prevent violent changes in our climate.'
Leonardo DiCaprio, Chairman, Earth Fair 2000

This book is about the contribution that economics can make to our understanding of environmental problems in the twenty-first century. DiCaprio's warning above is a timely reminder that the general public, as well as scientists and conservationists, have a responsibility to understand the dangers facing the planet and to act accordingly. Economics will play a key role in this process as the following chapters will demonstrate.

- Chapter 1 summarizes some of the recent developments in discussions about the state of the environment and reviews the questions economists ask about the environment.

- Chapter 2 examines the economic causes of environmental problems.

- Chapter 3 continues with these themes and discusses, for example, what is meant by 'efficient' pollution.

- Chapter 4 explores the relationship between economic growth and environmental damage.

- Chapter 5 looks at the question of how we measure the value of environmental benefits and the costs of environmental damage.

- Chapter 6 shows how we can use these calculations of costs and benefits for particular projects to decide on the amount of resources needed to save and improve the environment.

- Chapters 7, 8 and 9 discuss the measures that can be taken to improve the management of environmental resources, from both theoretical and practical standpoints, with reference to UK, European Union and international experience.

Chapter One
The environment and the economy

'I shot an arrow in the air. It stuck!'
Tom Lehrer, songwriter and mathematician

Preliminaries

The state of the world environment may provoke wry jokes of the kind quoted above, but there is also a genuine widespread concern. The publication in 2001 of Bjorn Lomborg's controversial book *The Skeptical Environmentalist* provoked a heated response and confirmed the continuing public interest in environmental issues. One of the more recent environmental catastrophes, the sinking of the tanker *Prestige* in November 2002 and the damage it inflicted on the Portuguese coastline, was yet another reminder of the impact of human activities on the health of the planet.

Oil killed 200,000 birds

PAUL BROWN AND JOHN VINCENT

The Prestige oil disaster killed about 200,000 birds from 71 species, making it one of the worst ecological disasters in the north-east Atlantic.

About a quarter of the victims were over-wintering birds from British and Irish coast breeding colonies, said the British Trust for Ornithology, which made the estimates from 21,500 birds recovered.

But the thickness of the oil from the tanker, which sank off Spain's Galicia coast in November, and the number of birds which sank in the sea or were bull-dozed by recovery teams, meant the casualties could be higher, possibly exceeding the worst recorded spill, the 1999 sinking of the Erika, off Brittany, which killed 300,000 birds.

The oldest birds known to have died include a 27-year-old great skua from Shetland, a 25-year-old guillemot from Scotland, and an Orkney puffin, 21. Many puffins, razorbills, gannets, great skuas and lesser black-backed gulls died. The worst hit colony was Great Saltee Island, Co Wexford, where 1,500 birds perished.

The Guardian, 7 March 2003

Throughout recent decades there has been a series of major incidents, caused by human activity, with far-reaching consequences for the environment. They have also affected public attitudes towards the environment. The incidents included:

Table 1 Examples of man-made incidents with major environmental consequences

Date	Incident	Description
1956	Windscale, England	Discharge of radioactive material
1966	Aberfan, Wales	Coal tip slide, 144 killed
1967	Torrey Canyon, England	Oil tanker, 119 000 tonnes crude oil spilt
1974	Flixborough, England	Vapour cloud explosion
1976	Seveso, Italy	Toxic chemical release
1978	Amoco Cadiz, France	Oil tanker, 223 000 tonnes crude oil spilt
1979	Three Mile Island, USA	Partial meltdown at nuclear plant
1979	Ixtoc, Gulf of Mexico	Oil platform, 531 000 tonnes crude oil spilt
1979	Atlantic Empress, Trinidad	Oil tanker, 287 000 tonnes crude oil spilt
1984	Bhopal, India	Gas leak, 3 800 killed
1986	Chernobyl, Ukraine	Explosion at nuclear power plant
1986	River Rhine	Chemical pollution
1989	Exxon Valdez, Alaska	Oil tanker, 37 000 tonnes crude oil spilt
1993	Braer, Scotland	Oil tanker, 85 000 tonnes light crude oil spilt
1995	Sea Empress, Wales	Oil tanker, 72 000 tonnes light crude oil spilt
1999	Tokaimura, Japan	Discharge of radioactive material
1999	Erika, France	Oil tanker, 26 000 tonnes fuel oil spilt
2002	Prestige, Portugal	Oil tanker, 12 000 tonnes fuel oil spilt

During this period there have also been less dramatic but arguably more serious man-made impacts on the environment which have posed significant challenges to governments and international organizations. Climate change and rising sea levels are perhaps the most obvious ones but the decline in **bio-diversity**, destruction of tropical rainforests, construction of large dams, acid rain, the Antarctic ozone hole, desertification and habitat loss are further problems which cause concern. The plight of the Aral Sea, often described as the world's worst environmental disaster, is a telling example of what can happen when governments get it wrong. Further instances include the mercury pollution of Minamata Bay in the 1950s, the toxic chemicals at Love Canal 1978, the collapse in the Grand Banks cod fishery in 1992, the controversial continuing use of DDT (an effective but persistent insecticide) in parts of the developing world and the outbreak of BSE (mad cow disease) in the UK in the 1980s followed by the foot and mouth epidemic of 2001.

Rachel Carson's book, *Silent Spring*, published in 1962, which drew attention to the long term effects of agro-chemicals, marked the beginning of the current worldwide concern for the human impact on the environment and established her as the founder of the modern environmental movement. At the time a reviewer for *Time* magazine criticized Carson's *'oversimplifications and downright errors'* and claimed that her *'scary generalizations'* were *'patently unsound'*. Nevertheless, *Silent Spring* provoked an international response which led eventually to the UN Conference on the Human Environment, held in Stockholm in early June 1972. The Stockholm meeting was the first global conference on the environment, indeed the first world conference to focus on a single issue. A series of books throughout the next few decades focused attention on population growth, **resource depletion** and environmental degradation. At this time campaigning pressure groups such as Greenpeace and Friends of the Earth were established to reflect growing public concern and to provide opportunities for active involvement. *Time* magazine nominated the Earth as its Man of the Year for 1988 and, in spite of its earlier doubts, selected Rachel Carson in 1999 as one of the most influential scientists and thinkers of the twentieth century and described her as the mother of modern environmentalism.

Carson therefore played a key role in the development of what Lomborg, a Danish professor of statistics, now describes as the '**Litany**' – the constant repetition of the claim that we are remorselessly plundering and damaging the environment. The essential core of Lomborg's argument is that the Litany is not backed up by the available evidence but that it has, nevertheless, gripped the public's imagination and attention. He cites four factors as being responsible for this: lopsided scientific research; institutional interests; the media's obsession with bad news; and our historical and perhaps biological predilection to welcome bad news. Lomborg's view seems to be that there has been a gigantic conspiracy between the environmental

Lomborg's litany

'We are all familiar with the Litany: the environment is in poor shape here on Earth. Our resources are running out. The population is ever growing, leaving less and less to eat. The air and the water are becoming ever more polluted. The planet's species are becoming extinct in vast numbers – we kill off more than 40,000 each year. The forests are disappearing, fish stocks are collapsing and the coral reefs are dying. We are defiling our Earth, the fertile topsoil is disappearing, we are paving over nature, destroying the wilderness, decimating the biosphere, and will end up killing ourselves in the process. The world's ecosystem is breaking down. We are fast approaching the absolute limit of viability, and the limits of growth are becoming apparent.'

Source: B. Lomborg, *The Skeptical Environmentalist*, CUP, 2001

community and the media to persuade a gullible public that the environment is being damaged beyond repair. The reality is, according to him, that things are getting better.

Needless to say, the publication of Lomborg's book created a huge controversy. *Scientific American* and the former Director General of the CBI dismissed its findings as flawed and inconsistent. *The Economist*, on the other hand, claimed that it was one of the most valuable books on public policy – not merely on environmental policy – to have been written for the intelligent general reader in the past ten years. On global warming, for example, it quotes Lomborg as showing that the cost of preventing it could easily outweigh the harm caused by letting it happen. Furthermore, in those countries likely to be most affected by global warming – the developing countries – he asserts that there would be much better ways of spending the money than on schemes designed to prevent it. As an illustration Lomborg claims that providing universal access to safe water would benefit more people than the small reduction in greenhouse gases proposed by the **Kyoto** treaty at a fifth of the price. In his own country, however, Lomborg's views were decidedly unpopular and were rejected by the Danish Ecological Council and the Danish Committees on Scientific Dishonesty which ruled that *The Skeptical Environmentalist* was contrary to the standards of good scientific practice.

Public opinion: according to Defra (Department for Environment, Food and Rural Affairs) the English public has consistently put environmental concerns high on the political agenda.

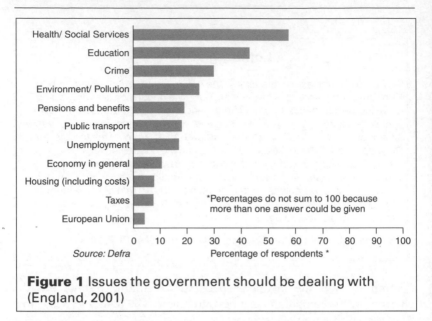

Figure 1 Issues the government should be dealing with (England, 2001)

Furthermore, as the following figure shows, it seems to have clear views about particular areas of the environment with waste disposal and pollution causing the most worries.

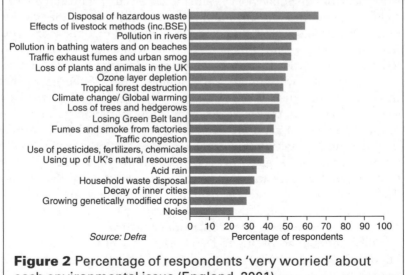

Figure 2 Percentage of respondents 'very worried' about each environmental issue (England, 2001)

The environment and opportunity cost

Although the issues in Figure 2 raise political and moral questions as well as complex scientific matters they all have one thing in common – *scarcity* – which also makes them economic questions. Economics is about the arrangements that societies make for the use and distribution of scarce resources. Environmental problems would not arise if there was an abundance of resources. There would be plentiful supplies of energy, raw materials and food. Most waste products could be easily and harmlessly disposed of if there were boundless oceans and atmosphere and there would be enough open spaces and countryside for everyone. However, there is no abundance of resources and many of our environmental problems occur simply because we have tended to treat the environment as a limitless resource.

Scarcity requires us to make choices, often very difficult ones, by comparing alternatives. If limited resources are fully employed more of something can only be obtained by having less of something else. So, for example, extra resources devoted to cleaning up the environment may mean fewer resources devoted to consumer goods.

This trade off is illustrated in Figure 3 with a simple **production possibility curve** (PPC) where consumer goods are measured on the

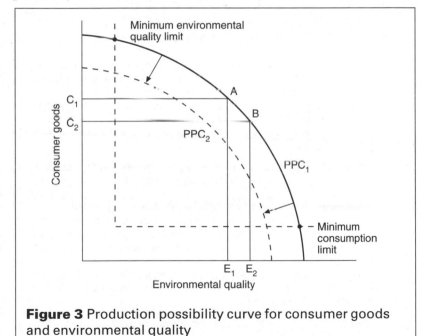

Figure 3 Production possibility curve for consumer goods and environmental quality

vertical axis and environmental quality is measured on the horizontal. Assuming fixed resources and constant technology, the curve PPC_1 shows the different combinations of these goods available to society. In practice a society would be most unlikely to opt for those points where the curve intersects either the vertical or horizontal axis because they would mean either no environmental protection at all or all resources devoted to the environment with no consumer goods. The realistic choices are indicated by that part of the PPC contained within the dotted quadrant.

If a society chooses point A on PPC_1 this corresponds to C_1 consumer goods and E_1 environmental quality. However, if it decides to raise environmental standards by moving to point B this requires a transfer of resources from consumer goods to the environment. This results in a reduction of consumer goods from C_1 to C_2 and an increase in environmental quality from E_1 to E_2. This reduction in consumer goods is known as the **opportunity cost** of environmental improvements, but when we consider the possible future impact of such a choice the cost may be quite tolerable. Consider for example the harmful long-term effect of environmental degradation on the

---

Protecting the environment

The government believes that economic prosperity and social progress must be achieved while protecting the environment, to ensure a better quality of life for everyone, today and for future generations. It is committed to tackling global problems, such as climate change, and to improving the local environment in Britain's towns, cities and rural areas. The Pre-Budget Report sets out new steps to improve the environment and urban areas, by:

- **improving support for environmentally-friendly waste disposal**, such as recycling, while continuing to support local community environmental projects
- **minimising the amount of waste sent to landfill**, an environmentally harmful form of disposal, by consulting on increases in the landfill tax
- **consulting on further reforms to promote cleaner fuels and transport** to improve air quality while maintaining a competitive economy; and
- **consulting on a new proposal to allow local authorities to spend increases in business rates revenue on local priorities**, including regeneration of urban areas.

Source: HM Treasury, Pre-Budget Report, November 2002

---

productivity of labour and agriculture. This could shift the PPC from PPC_1 to PPC_2 thus reducing all combinations of consumer goods and environmental quality. If society is concerned about the well being of future generations, then it would be appropriate to locate at point B, which corresponds to a sustainable level of consumer goods and a high level of environmental protection, which would maintain the original PPC intact.

Whereas the shape of the PPC is, in the short run, determined by the quantity and quality of resources and technology, the actual location on the curve is decided by public preferences and the political process.

Questions which economists ask

Economists enable societies to make better and more efficient choices about environmental issues by asking probing questions about all aspects of a particular decision. These questions are:

- What is the opportunity cost of achieving a particular environmental outcome?
- Is the environmental objective – for example, increasing the amount of **renewable energy** – being achieved in the most **cost effective** way? Failure to do so would mean that society is operating inefficiently at some point inside its PPC.
- What are the most suitable instruments for encouraging cost-effective solutions?
- How do societies value different aspects of the environment, and how can they be certain that the right balance is struck between **costs** and **benefits**?
- How are the needs of future generations taken into account when making decisions about the environment?

These are just some of the themes which will be addressed in subsequent chapters. If such questions are neglected then an over-zealous 'green at any price' approach may result, which would be wasteful and ultimately harmful to the environment. The inescapable scarcity of resources forces societies to make hard and difficult choices about the environment as it does in other areas of public activity.

KEY WORDS
Bio-diversity   Opportunity cost Resource depletion   Renewable energy Litany   Cost effective Kyoto   Costs and benefits Production possibility curve

Further reading

Carson R., *Silent Spring*, Penguin Books, 2000

Grant, S., and Vidler, C., Section 3.6 in Economics AS for AQA, Heinemann, 2003

Hanley N. et al., Chapter 1, *Introduction to Environmental Economics*, OUP, 2001

Lomborg B., Part 1, *The Skeptical Environmentalist*, CUP, 2001

Useful websites

http://www.lomborg.com/critique.htm
http://www.greenpeace.org.uk/
http://www.foe.co.uk/
http://www.environment-agency.gov.uk/
http://www.defra.gov.uk/
http://www.bized.ac.uk
http://www.unep.org/

Data response question

Read the following extracts from the Assessment and Qualifications Alliance paper, January 2002. Then answer the questions that follow.

Extract A

Storms brewing

Britain has done much to cut greenhouse gases — but it's still not enough. The climate change programme published yesterday by the government, continues to make the UK one of the most progressive countries attending the environmental conference at The Hague.

It includes policies that would cut the UK's greenhouse gas emissions (5 by 23 per cent below 1990 levels by 2010 — almost double the legally binding targets agreed at previous conferences.

But the programme acknowledges that cuts of 60 to 70 per cent globally may be necessary in the long term.

Meanwhile, a Scottish strategy has set targets for producing 18 per (10)
cent of Scotland's electricity from renewable resources instead of non-
renewable ones by 2010, spending millions on public transport,
promoting liquid-petroleum gas and improving energy efficiency in
buildings.

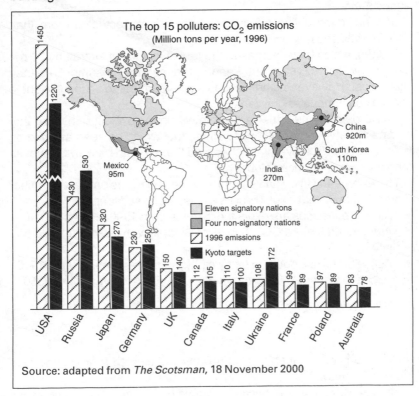

The top 15 polluters: CO_2 emissions
(Million tons per year, 1996)

China 920m
South Korea 110m
Mexico 95m
India 270m

Eleven signatory nations
Four non-signatory nations
1996 emissions
Kyoto targets

USA 1450 / 1220
Russia 530 / 430
Japan 320 / 270
Germany 230 / 250
UK 150 / 140
Canada 112 / 105
Italy 110 / 100
Ukraine 108 / 172
France 99 / 89
Poland 97 / 89
Australia 83 / 78

Source: adapted from *The Scotsman*, 18 November 2000

Extract B

Sky-high pollution from the fastest way to travel

Flying from Glasgow to Miami causes as much pollution as the total
annual mileage of the average British car driver. Air travel, as the fastest
growing and most polluting form of transport, is a major contributor to
global warming.

Aeroplanes alone generate 3 per cent of damaging emissions, such as (5)
carbon dioxide (CO_2), the principal global warming gas, and it has been
predicted this could rise to l0–20 per cent by 2005. Significantly, jet
emissions are deposited directly into the upper atmosphere, where CO_2

can linger for up to a century.

The tell-tale vapour trails that planes etch across the skies are also (1 believed to affect the formation of high-level cirrus clouds, which may change the delicate balance between heat entering and leaving the atmosphere.

Concern is mounting because air travel is expected to more than double within the next 15 years. (1!

Airlines, which have increased the fuel efficiency of aircraft by 70 per cent in the last 40 years, are keen to reduce fuel consumption – their major cost. However, rising fuel costs alone appear to be insufficient to reduce consumption significantly.

Unlike petrol, airline fuel is completely untaxed. Politicians fear that (2(adding an environmental levy to airline fuel would be seen as a tax on holidays. The UK Government has said that it would back the move, as long as it was introduced globally.

The European Union has supported taxes on flights between member states, but fears that it could put its airlines at a disadvantage. (2!

- Aircraft emissions are expected to treble from 1990 levels by 2015.
- Airliners emit more CO_2 than all of Britain's vehicles, industries and homes.
- Airline travel has doubled every eight years, on average, since 1960.
- Aircraft produce 2.4% of man-made CO_2, rising to over 7% by 2050. (3(

Source: adapted from *The Scotsman*, 18 November 2000

1. (a) What is meant by an 'environmental levy' (Extract B, line 21)? [4 marks]
   (b) Distinguish between 'renewable' and 'non-renewable' resources (Extract A lines 11–12). [6 marks]
2. What economic changes are likely to have caused airline travel to have doubled every eight years, on average, since 1960 (Extract B, line 29)? [6 marks]
3. The chart in Extract A shows that the USA is the single largest CO_2 polluter. Does this necessarily mean that large polluters such as the USA are 'dirty' countries with inefficient industries? Justify your answer. [6 marks]
4. With the help of a supply and demand diagram, explain how a tax on airline fuel would be likely to affect air travel. [8 marks]

5. The data suggest that international agreement would be necessary to implement an international tax on airline fuel. Identify and evaluate alternative policies that could be used in order to reduce global warming caused by air travel. [20 marks]
   [Q2, AQA, Unit 3, January 2002]

Chapter Two

Economic causes of environmental problems

'*The closed Earth of the future requires economic principles which are somewhat different from the open Earth of the past.*'
Kenneth Boulding

Introduction
Since it is so harmful, how is it that we allow environmental damage to happen? Of course, some environmental disturbance is unavoidable. Even the most basic level of human existence – breathing, eating, defecating – has an impact on our surroundings. Almost every activity from farming to travel makes demands upon, and pollutes, the environment. *Zero rates of extraction and pollution are not an answer.* The solution lies, rather, in conducting our economies and ourselves so as to minimize this impact. The ways in which this might be done are discussed in the remainder of the book. In this and the following chapters we ask an essential preliminary question: how does *avoidable* environmental damage occur in the first place?

A new model of the economy
To help us answer this we need a relevant model of the economy. The conventional circular flow model (Figure 4), familiar to students of macro-economics, shows *on the lower loop* the flow of output between producers and households; and *on the upper loop* the flow of inputs to producers.

Although this model is useful, it has a serious limitation. Even if international trade is included it is still, in a wider meaning of the term, a '*closed*' model. It takes no account of the interaction between the economy and environment on which it depends. This is also shown in Figure 4, with environmental connections added below the circular flow model.

The environment, represented in the lower part of the diagram, performs three functions:
- it provides resources
- it offers amenities
- it absorbs waste.

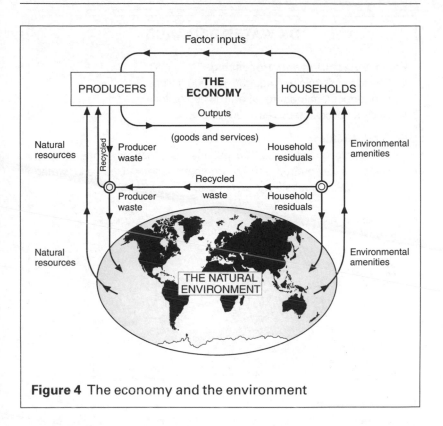

Figure 4 The economy and the environment

The flow of natural resources – minerals, water, energy, plant and animal life – from the environment to producers is shown on the extreme left of the diagram. This flow contributes in turn to the output of goods and services going to households. On the far right of the diagram we see, flowing directly to households, environmental amenities in the form of country walks, pleasant views and the opportunity for other recreational activities. Producers and households generate 'leftovers' or residuals, some of which are recycled to contribute once more to the flow of output. The remainder are dumped in the environment – labelled 'producer and household waste' in the diagram.

The three functions of the environment – as a provider of resources and of amenities and as an absorber of waste – interact with each other, sometimes in a competitive way and sometimes in a complementary way. Water is a good illustration of this.

The data in the boxed item opposite show competing claims on water use in the UK. We can summarize the problem with a simple

UK WATER DEMANDS

For manufacturing and processing
- One ton of aluminium requires 300 000 gallons.
- A four-door family car requires 100 000 gallons.
- One bag of coke requires 3000 gallons.

For households
- Two-thirds of the 3.8 billion gallons used daily in England and Wales is accounted for by domestic users. Domestic water consumption breaks down as follows:

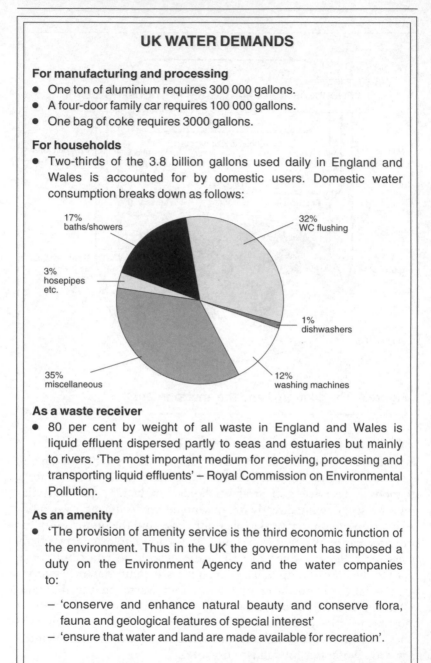

17% baths/showers

32% WC flushing

3% hosepipes etc.

1% dishwashers

35% miscellaneous

12% washing machines

As a waste receiver
- 80 per cent by weight of all waste in England and Wales is liquid effluent dispersed partly to seas and estuaries but mainly to rivers. 'The most important medium for receiving, processing and transporting liquid effluents' – Royal Commission on Environmental Pollution.

As an amenity
- 'The provision of amenity service is the third economic function of the environment. Thus in the UK the government has imposed a duty on the Environment Agency and the water companies to:

  – 'conserve and enhance natural beauty and conserve flora, fauna and geological features of special interest'
  – 'ensure that water and land are made available for recreation'.

Sources: Welsh Water plc; Water Services Association

hypothetical example. The Rubicon River, as it flows into a populated area, provides water for industrial, agricultural and domestic services; this same water is discharged back into the Rubicon as effluent; and citizens of Rubiconia City like to spend their leisure time engaging in water sports and fishing. There is a limit to the capacity of the Rubicon to fulfil any one of these functions and it may be further reduced by its use for other purposes. Whether or not these uses are mutually exclusive will frequently depend on the level of use and the level of water in the river. High rates of effluent discharged, especially when the river level is low, would mean that for some purposes the water of the Rubicon could not be used as production input and it would certainly reduce its amenity services. When the river level is high, however, its ability to break down and absorb a given level of waste is increased and the diluted effluent is no longer a serious threat to other functions.

The spaceship economy

The new model, which incorporates the interaction between the economy and the environment, helps us to see more clearly why things go wrong. In both our imaginary example and in reality, a river may become poisoned with waste, reduced to a sluggish trickle through excessive water use, or become so crowded with recreational users that it ceases to be enjoyable. Figure 4 shows why the river, or any other environmental resource, is misused. The vital links between the economy and the environment in the diagram are, for reasons explained in the following sections, somehow forgotten or overlooked, *so decisions taken in the economy about making the best use of resources pay little regard to the environment.*

Because the environmental links do not appear in market prices, in the balance sheets of producers, or in the calculations of national income, we tend to regard the environment as if it were a free resource. In an influential article 'The Coming Spaceship Earth', the American economist Kenneth Boulding claimed that many of our environmental problems arose because we tended to treat the world as a 'cowboy economy' with a limitless 'wild west' frontier of resources available for reckless exploitation. By contrast, as we come to realize our impact on the environment, we should think of our planet *'as a spaceship, without unlimited reservoirs of anything, either for extraction or for pollution'.*

Market failure

The great advantage of markets, when they are working properly, is that they ensure an efficient use of scarce resources. Markets generate

17

THERMODYNAMICS

Central to the view of the Earth as a system with limited resources is the famous *First Law of Thermodynamics,* which states that energy and matter cannot be created or destroyed. In terms of our new model this implies that, if we wish to reduce the polluting mass of waste disposed of in the natural environment, the options open to us might be to:

- produce fewer goods and services
- reduce the amount of residuals generated in the production and use of goods and services
- increase recycling.

Energy cannot be destroyed, but the *Second Law of Thermodynamics* (entropy) tells us what happens – it is dissipated or transformed. The economy draws upon usable, low-entropy materials – minerals and fuel – from the environment. In turn, manufacturing and consumption generate less usable (sometimes useless) higher-entropy waste products, gases and wasted heat. This reminds us that, despite the scope for recycling, it can never be completely successful. Recycling itself uses energy and creates further waste. *100 per cent recycling is not economically feasible or socially desirable.*

There are three sets of economic reasons why in mixed economies (government sector plus private markets) we manage to ignore the lessons of thermodynamics and overlook the links between the economy and the environment:

- **market failure** (discussed in this chapter)
- **missing markets** (discussed in Chapter 3)
- **government failure** (discussed in Chapter 3).

information on scarcity, which is signalled in the form of prices. At the same time, prices provide powerful incentives to act on this information, while suppliers of capital and labour, in seeking to avoid losses and maximize income, try to make the best use of their resources.

Nevertheless, the wasteful destruction of scarce environmental resources is an example of a **market failure.** Whenever a price becomes distorted or misleading, so that it does not provide a true signal of the underlying forces of supply and demand, then market failure occurs. Too much or too little is produced. The artificially high prices caused by monopolies are just one example.

Here we are concerned with the impact on the environment of market failure caused by *externalities*. These are so named because they are costs (called **negative externalities** or **external costs**), or benefits (**positive externalities** or **external benefits**), which extend beyond – and are therefore *external* to – the actions of a particular supplier or consumer. Thus the act of one household or firm imposes external costs or confers external benefits on another household or firm. These external costs or benefits are not transmitted through prices.

Both positive and negative externalities can arise between producers, between consumers, or between producers and consumers, as shown in Table 2 overleaf.

Negative externalities

Figure 5 illustrates a negative externality. It might, for example, be the cost of acid rain, damaging to forestry and fishing, created by sulphur dioxide fumes from coal-fired power stations. The acid rain damage is shown as MEC, the marginal external cost curve – the damage caused

---

DIRTY WASHING

The effect of smoke from a factory chimney was one of the earliest textbook cases of a negative externality: quoted by the economist A.C. Pigou, whose pioneering study *Economics of Welfare* was published in 1920. Based on an actual investigation in Manchester in 1914, this showed that households in the vicinity of the factory incurred costs of £290 000, caused by soot falling on washing hanging out to dry.

Today, in an era of washing machines, we would concentrate on studying the more injurious effects of emissions listed in Table 2. However, the principle which Pigou identified applies to all cases of pollution: the difference between **private costs** (in this case the cost of manufacturing and of inputs purchased by the factory) and **social costs** (the total cost to the community of the factory output). This should include the external cost of £290 000 for laundry bills. Because the laundry costs are external to the firm, they are not included in its bills or cost accounts – and therefore in the price it charges.

Private cost + external cost = social cost.

Remember that the so-called private costs must be included because the resources the factory output absorbs are not available to the wider community for any alternative use.

Table 2 Examples of environmental externalities

	Negative (cost)	Positive (benefit)
Consumer to consumer	• Car exhaust fumes/noise • Traffic congestion • Street litter, especially from take-aways	• Well-kept gardens are a pleasure to passers-by and raise the value of adjacent properties
Producer to producer	• A crop spray used on a potato farm which also kills insects that pollinate fruit trees in neighbouring orchards • Depletion of fish stocks	• A farmer improving land drainage may at the same time improve adjacent land on other farms
Producer to consumer	• Any waste or emission dumped or discharged in the environment without taking account of the external costs	• Any pleasant aroma from a coffee or chocolate factory, perfumery or bakery

by an extra unit of output. It is assumed that the power stations have a fixed technology and can only alter emissions by reducing output. The curve is upward sloping as for most types of pollution, because the damage to forests and fisheries becomes worse at an increasing rate. At certain levels of pollution, for example, all fish in a river may die.

The supply curve, assuming a perfectly competitive industry, is S, which is derived from the horizontal sum of the marginal private cost curves (MPC) of the firms in the industry. The demand curve D is, at the same time, also a measure of how much the community is willing to pay for an extra unit of output from the power stations – the marginal social benefit (MSB = D). The competitive industry produces the output which maximizes profits, where supply is equal to demand – output Q_c at price P_c. From a social viewpoint, this price is too low and the output too high. It takes no account of the external costs. To do this we must add MEC to S (putting MEC on top of the S curve). We then get a full measure of marginal social costs – the MSC curve.

$$MSC = MEC + MPC.$$

The **socially efficient output** (which can also be called the socially optimum output) is at the point where the price P_s of the product is equal to the marginal social cost of production at output Q_s. This is efficient because at this point the extra cost of the extra or marginal

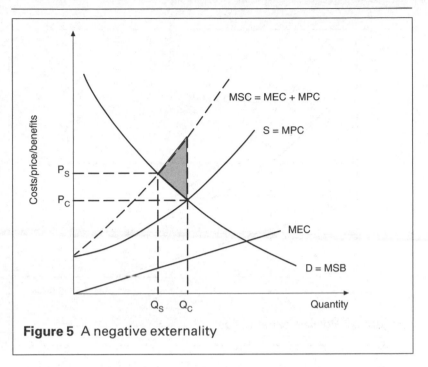

Figure 5 A negative externality

unit of output, including environmental costs, is just equal to what the community thinks it is worth – its price, P_S = MSC. But the competitive industry produces an output Q_C at which point the price P_C is less than the MSC. This tells us that output is too high and too much sulphur dioxide is being discharged into the atmosphere.

The cost of the inefficiency is the shaded area – all units of output for which MSC exceeds MSB (known as a **welfare triangle loss**). This is a loss without any compensating gains, and represents the full costs associated with that part of the output between Q_S and Q_C for which the community is not prepared to pay. Nevertheless, it is inflicted on the community because the price P_C is too low – hiding the external cost. The efficient level of output is at Q_S at a price P_S.

Positive externalities

Figure 6 shows how the consequences of positive externalities may be a level of output which is too low, and takes the example of a home-owner's garden.

The marginal cost curve (MC) for the investment of time and money in gardening is horizontal because the extra (or marginal) costs to the house-holder of planting an extra bed of flowers, it is assumed, will not

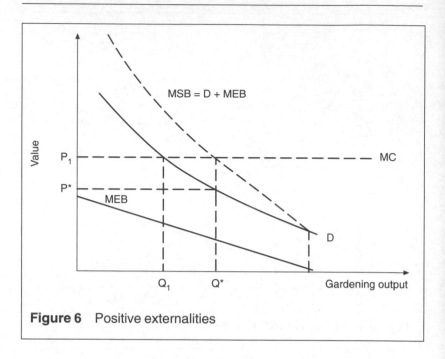

Figure 6 Positive externalities

be affected by the amount of gardening done. The pleasant garden generates external benefits to neighbours and passers-by, as the marginal external benefit curve (MEB) shows. This curve is likely to be downwards sloping in this case, because the marginal benefit may be large for small improvements to a very untidy garden, but less significant as further work is done.

The marginal social benefit (MSB) curve is calculated by adding the **marginal private benefit** and the marginal external benefit together – putting the MEB curve on top of the demand curve D. Thus:

$$MSB = MPB + MEB.$$

The efficient level of output Q^* is at the point where the marginal social benefit to the community of an 'extra unit' of gardening improvements is equal to the marginal cost of the work. This is where the MC and MSB curves intersect. The inefficiency occurs because the home-owner does not manage to reap all the benefits from the investment in the garden improvements. Passers-by cannot be charged for the benefit they derive from pleasant gardens, nor then is there any way of reaping the gains from the impact on other property values. Consequently the price P_1 is too high to achieve the appropriate level of garden maintenance for the neighbourhood. The efficient price would be P*, a pleasing thought for gardeners.

Suburban gardens may seem a trivial example, compared with world-wide environmental problems, but the principle established here has wider implications. *Wherever a positive externality occurs, not enough resources or effort will be directed towards producing the right amount of the good or activity which generates the positive externality.*

Remedies
How can market failure caused by externalities be remedied? This is discussed in more detail in Chapters 7, 8 and 9. Here we briefly note two possibilities.

Regulations
Regulations could be imposed by the government restricting output to Q_s in Figure 5 — this is known as a **command and control system** (CAC).

A market incentive approach
This involves using the price signal to obtain the socially efficient output. This could be achieved by a tax on the polluting output (originally proposed by Pigou — hence the **Pigouvian tax**). If the tax raises the price from P_c to P_s, output is reduced to the desired level Q_s. The Pigouvian tax is a measure which is consistent with the **polluter pays principle** (PPP) — the idea that the price should include all external environmental costs. A sound idea this may be, but put into practice in the form advocated by its most enthusiastic supporters it could lead to some controversially high prices — for example, £1.38 for a hamburger (see boxed item). Read this now and *try the following questions when you have read Chapter 3:*

● How does this article illustrate both government and market failure?
● What economic principle is being proposed here?
● What are the practical problems of such an idea?

Human action inevitably causes some environmental disturbance and damage. However, much of the environmental destruction that occurs is unnecessary and avoidable. It arises in part because of the failure of markets to provide the right price signals so as to minimize the environmentally harmful effects of pollution and consumption (negative externalities), or to encourage the good effects (positive externalities).

Why a hamburger should cost $200

NANCY DUNNE

Ecologists ... believe the world's trade ministers can only tinker with an economic system that is fundamentally flawed by its failure to count the ecological costs of production. 'This could leave us with a world where there's lots of money but dirty air and water and environmental degradation,' says Alan Thein Durning, author of *Saving the Forests: What Will it Take?* from the Worldwatch Institute, an environmental group. What is needed is a system of 'full-cost pricing' that includes environmental costs in production of goods, he says. This would radically alter cost structures.

A mature forest tree in India would then be worth $50,000 (£34,000), according to the Centre for Science and Environment in New Delhi. A hamburger produced on pasture cleared from rain forests would cost $200. One hectare of a Malaysian forest, providing carbon storage services and helping to prevent climate change, would be worth more than $3,000 over the long term, according to Durning.

Environmentalists fear the costs of not moving towards ecological pricing will only become clear after it is too late. Deforestation is accelerating; two-thirds of the planet's original forests have already disappeared.

Political reform is also necessary to reforestation efforts. 'To varying degrees, a bond between timber money and political power is found in all the world's main timber economies,' says Durning. 'In less democratic societies, those who question the prerogatives of economic power all too often end up as murder statistics in human rights reports.'

Durning alleges that in countries like Malaysia – the world's largest exporter of tropical timber – elected leaders distribute to their loyal supporters contracts for the exploitation of public resources. Even in the US, the government moves reluctantly against the entrenched timber, mining and beef interests.

He would like full-cost pricing phased in over 10–20 years through user fees, green taxes and tariffs. He reckons that a $3-a-day charge to visitors to US national forests would raise more money than timber sales from US government-owned lands. But first, governments must stop subsidizing forest destruction.

No country can move to full cost pricing alone without risking having their industries undercut by foreign producers whose governments do not make environmental destruction costly. Global action is necessary.

Financial Times 12 January 1994

In addition to market failure we must consider the problems created by missing markets and government failure, which are discussed in the following chapter.

KEY WORDS

Market failure	Social costs
Missing markets	Socially efficient output
Negative externalities	Welfare triangle loss
External costs	Marginal private benefit
Positive externalities	Command/control system
External benefits	Pigouvian tax
Private costs	Polluter pays principle

Further reading
Bamford, C., Chapter 3 in *Transport Economics*, 3rd edn, Heinemann Educational, 2001

Grant, S., and Vidler, C., Section 3.6 in *Economics AS for AQA*, Heinemann, 2003

Munday, S., Chapter 4 in *Markets and Market Failure*, Heinemann, 2000

Nixon, F., Chapter 6 in *Development Economics*, 2nd edn, Heinemann, 2001

Useful websites
Greenpeace: www.greenpeace.org.uk/
Friends of the Earth: www.foe.org.uk/

Essay topics
1. (a) Define, and give examples of, external costs and benefits. [10 marks]
   (b) Discuss whether it is possible to achieve an optimal allocation of resources of externalities. [10 marks]
2. (a) Distinguish, with the aid of examples, between positive externalities and negative externalities. [10 marks]
   (b) Discuss the extent to which subsidies to producers are the best means for a government to encourage the consumption of goods and services that generate positive externalities. [15 marks]

Data response question

This task is taken from a specimen question set by OCR in 2002. Read the extracts then answer the questions.

Government and the environment

There are several serious concerns about our environment. These include pollution of various sorts, the effects of global warming and fears over the future of the countryside.

All environmental problems can be seen as examples of market failure. They are problems created by some individuals and groups that impact upon others who are not involved in the decision-making. As such, these problems may require government action if they are to be tackled. The following article considers the government's recent record in tackling some of these issues.

Promises, promises:
has Blair really been a friend of the environment?

When Tony Blair made his final speech to voters before the 1997 general election, the Labour leader promised to put the environment at the 'heart of government'.

After Labour's victory, each government department was given its own 'green minister' and a Commons Select Committee was set up to provide proper scrutiny of environmental issues. How has the government matched up to its early promises? (5

Fuel prices
The Environment Minister, Michael Meacher, had said the automatic fuel escalator (which significantly raised taxes on petrol each year) was (10 valuable both in persuading people to use public transport and in helping to reduce pollution. Unfortunately, the huge rise in the price of crude oil in 2000 left the government vulnerable to fuel protests by lorry drivers and farmers. Ministers panicked and opted for cuts in duty on diesel for hauliers without any additional environmental safeguards. (15

Climate change
Deputy Prime Minister, John Prescott, took a leading role in the agreement at the Kyoto climate summit in 1997 to reduce greenhouse gas emissions that cause global warming. However, by abandoning the fuel duty escalator and pandering to the haulage industry, greenhouse (20 gas emissions are likely to increase.

Wildlife and the countryside
The Countryside and Rights of Way Act introduced the so-called 'right to

roam'. This allows visitors to the countryside to walk freely on all footpaths. There has also been action to defend peatlands from the (25) destructive actions of fertilizer companies, and tough talk (but no legislation) about excessive leaks from water company pipes.

Nuclear power
Tony Blair has given the nuclear industry strong support since taking office. He believes that the industry offers crucial jobs and skills in the (30) depressed west Cumbrian region.

Renewable energy
It is believed that renewable energy creates less pollution as well as providing a sustainable energy source. The government announced a target of 10 per cent of total energy generation from renewable sources (35) by 2010. A subsidy of £100 million for solar, wind, wave and biomass forms of power generation has recently been announced but many experts claim wind power should be boosted with bigger capital grants.

Source: adapted from *The Independent,* 7 March 2001

1. (a) Define the term 'externality'. [2 marks]
   (b) From the article, identify two examples of a negative externality. [2 marks]
   (c) From the article, identify two examples of a positive externality. [2 marks]
2. The newspaper article talks about a large increase in fuel prices (lines 9–15).
   (a) Give one group who might suffer financial hardship due to a large rise in fuel prices. Explain the reasons for your answer. [3 marks]
   (b) Give one type of transport business that might benefit through a large increase in fuel prices. Explain the reasons for your answer. [3 marks]
3. (a) State two characteristics of 'public goods'. [2 marks]
   (b) How far does the 'right to roam' (line 23) make the countryside more like a public good? [4 marks]
4. (a) Define the term 'subsidy'. [2 marks]
   (b) Using a diagram, explain how a government subsidy paid to the renewable energy industry might increase the consumption of renewable energy. [7 marks]
   (c) Identify and comment on the costs and benefits of paying a large subsidy to the renewable energy industry. [8 marks]
5. Discuss the advantages and disadvantages to the government in using taxes to improve the quality of the environment. [10 marks]
[Q1, OCR, Paper 2882, May 2002]

Chapter Three

Efficient pollution, missing markets and government failure

The phrase 'efficient pollution' enrages some Greens and further convinces them that economists are completely insensitive to the environment.

The phrase **'efficient pollution'** appears to contain a contradiction because pollution is clearly harmful and it might seem absurd to imagine that it could also be efficient. Yet this is simply a statement about making the best use of scarce resources. As Figure 5 on page 21 showed, even at the socially efficient level of output Q_s, some pollution from sulphur emissions will occur. This is not surprising since zero pollution would require no production, which might be quite unacceptable.

What is the efficient level of pollution? This can be seen more clearly from Figure 7(a) which just concentrates on the costs of the damage done by the pollution and the cost of reducing it (**abatement costs**). That includes the cost of pollution control equipment; the cost of inspection and the value of any output forgone in reducing emissions. The **marginal cost of abatement** (MCA) curve shows the extra cost of abatement arising from the reduction in pollution by one unit – measured here by the level of emissions. To understand the diagram, consider a movement from right to left – a reduction in pollution levels.

The steepness of the MCA curve will vary according to the type of pollutant. The MCA curve for reducing wastes discharged into a river, for example, will be different from that for lowering emissions of sulphur dioxide into the atmosphere. Nevertheless, the extra (or marginal) cost of extra reductions in pollution can be expected to rise as more valuable resources are drawn into further abatement. The marginal cost may become very high at low levels of pollution. Increasing the quality of river water from 85 to 95 per cent purity, it has been estimated, *may double abatement costs*. Similarly, totally litter-free streets, requiring a warden on every street corner, may be prohibitively expensive.

The **marginal social cost of pollution** (MSCP) curve measures the costs created by an increase in pollution of one unit – a movement to the right on the diagram. It is the same as the MEC curve of Figure 5,

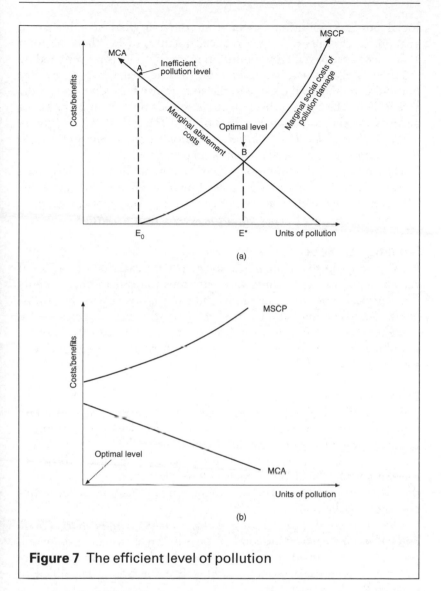

Figure 7 The efficient level of pollution

but relabelled to remind us that we are only talking about marginal social costs arising from pollution. The MSCP curve is sometimes zero up to a certain pollution level because of the capacity of the environment to absorb waste – by natural dispersion, by wind, water and bio-degradation.

The socially efficient level of pollution is at E^*, where the marginal social cost of pollution is equal to the marginal social cost of abatement. If emissions were reduced further, to E_0, then the total abatement cost of reducing pollution from E^* to E_0 is represented by the area E^*E_0AB. The value of reducing the damage done by this pollution, and hence the value to the community for reducing it, is the area E^*E_0B. The costs of this reduction exceeds the benefit by E_0AB – a net loss for the community. *Any point to the left of E^* will be an inefficiently high level of pollution reduction since the marginal cost to the community will exceed the marginal benefit.*

The case of lethal pollutants, which are potentially threatening on a worldwide scale, such as CFCs, is shown in Figure 7(b). Here the MSCP is above the abatement cost curve at every level of emission. *In this case the efficient level of pollution is zero, at zero output.*

Missing markets

How exactly do the problems associated with externalities arise? If each firm had to pay to emit fumes into the atmosphere, then socially efficient decisions would be made. But since no one owns the atmosphere, there is no market and therefore no market price for clean air to guide businesses' and consumers' decisions. Firms have every incentive to pollute because clean air is mistakenly regarded as a *free good* with a price of zero.

Property rights

The connection between missing markets and the absence of property rights was first analysed by the Nobel Prize winning economist, Ronald Coase. If resources are not owned, they will be wasted because no price will be charged for their use. Coase argued that if property rights are well defined, individuals will benefit by bargaining for use of the scarce resources – **Coase bargaining** as it is sometimes called – thus creating a market.

This internalizes the externality which is included in the market price and ensures an efficient outcome. A possible answer to environmental problems, it is claimed, would be to extend and clearly define property rights in all natural resources. The scope for this is examined in Chapter 8.

The problems created by the absence of property rights can be shown in the following example. If fishermen have unlimited access to waters which nobody owns (Figure 8), each trawler will catch fish at a rate of C_1 and where marginal private cost (MPC) is equal to demand – assuming perfect competition in the fishing industry. If competition and modern technology cause the total catch of fish to rise beyond the

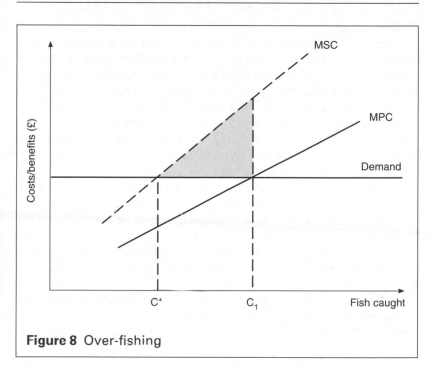

Figure 8 Over-fishing

natural replenishment level, stocks of fish and the fishing industry will eventually cease to exist. Although this is recognized, each individual firm feels that its catch is too small to make any difference. Competing trawlers will try to catch as many fish as possible while stocks last, so creating an externality by contributing to the extinction of the stock.

The marginal social cost curve (MSC), which includes the external costs of excessive fishing, indicates that the socially efficient level of catch would be C^*, where MSC equals demand. Individual trawlers, ignoring external cost, catch too many fish at C_1. The shaded area represents the external cost of over-fishing. If the property rights in the fishery were created and placed in the hands of a single owner, the problem might be solved. It is in the owner's interest to charge a fee to fishermen equal to the marginal social cost of fishing. This reduces the catch to C^*, which preserves stocks and the industry.

A practical problem arising from the solution suggested above is to exclude fishermen who don't pay. This might be feasible with the private ownership of a small river or lake, but impossible for the single owner of a vast resource such as an ocean. Some form of international co-operation with government regulation of the fishing industry may be necessary.

Public goods

The difficulty of *exclusion* is common to what are known as **public goods.** A public good is a type of good that may be supplied by private enterprise or the public sector, but usually has to be financed by the public sector. With a **private good,** such as ice cream, people who don't pay can be *excluded.* Also, consumption is rival – one person's ice cream consumption means less for others. By contrast a public good, such as a lighthouse, is *non-rival* – an extra ship does not affect the availability of light for other ships. It is also *non-excludable* – no vessel can be denied the benefit of the light.

The quality of the environment is also a form of public good. If, for example, the purity of air is improved in an industrial area, everyone benefits because no one can be excluded. But if we depended on the voluntary payments to secure clean air, people would be tempted to become **free-riders,** relying on the payments of others. Consequently, a private firm undertaking to purify the air will probably not earn enough revenue to cover the costs.

It follows from this that *private markets, if left entirely to themselves, are likely to under-supply improvements in environmental quality.* Although there is demand for, and a capacity to supply, environmental goods, the necessary markets are incomplete or missing. Some form of collective finance through taxation rather than individual voluntary payments may be necessary.

Congestion and public goods – traffic jams

When the use of a public good approaches capacity – a crowded national park or road network for example – it ceases to be non-rival. It becomes an **'impure' public good,** with rival consumption, one of the features of a private good. Well below full capacity, an extra walker or motorist will have no effect on the consumption of other users. Also in terms of wear and tear, the marginal cost caused by extra use is virtually zero. Apart from the exclusion problem, this is often seen as a justification for not charging for public goods. Economic efficiency requires that marginal cost (zero in this case) equals price.

However, at peak times each extra walker or motorist, by adding to congestion, reduces the utility of others, so creating a marginal cost quite distinct from wear and tear. This is shown in Figure 9. At off-peak times, the marginal cost (MC) and average cost (AC) of travelling, measured in the value of driving time, are equal. At any point up to V_1, an extra car can join the traffic without slowing down other drivers, but beyond V_1 congestion increases as each driver causes a time delay for others. Since

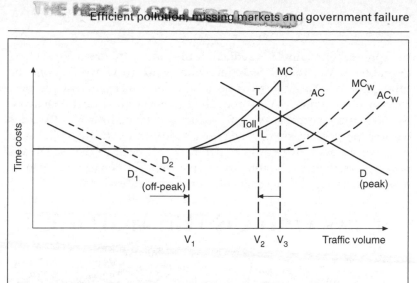

Figure 9 Congestion externalities – a traffic problem

average cost (measured in average journey time) is rising, the marginal cost, or addition to total journey time of all vehicles together, is above average cost.

Suppose for example the average journey time for each of 19 vehicles travelling the same way between two points on a particular road is 60 minutes. If an extra vehicle, by adding to congestion, increases average journey time for all vehicles by 5 minutes, then the total extra time inflicted on all other road users is $19 \times 5 = 95$ minutes. Including the time of the twentieth motorist, the increase in total journey time for all vehicles, that is the extra or marginal cost, is $95 + 65 = 160$ minutes, well above the average time of 65 minutes. Because much of this marginal cost, known as a **congestion externality**, is borne by other motorists, each additional driver entering a congested road, thinks only of increases in average journey time. Consequently demand increases to V_3 – an excessively congested and inefficient level of traffic, where marginal social cost exceeds marginal social benefit. A road-widening scheme will reduce journey time but may create congestion externalities once again at an even higher volume of traffic as demand expands (dotted MC_W and AC_W in Figure 9). For example, the London orbital road (M25) was designed for about 80 thousand cars a day; but now its busiest section (in the south-west) carries up to 200 thousand a day.

This is another example of a missing market and missing market price, which is needed to internalize the congestion externality and bring marginal social cost into equality with marginal social benefit. A charge or toll for peak-period use could be the answer.

Suppose, for example, a reduction in peak traffic from V_3 to V_2 is desirable. At V_2 a toll, at peak times only, equal to TL would bring the total price of using the road up to the full marginal cost: drivers' average driving time (LV_2) + the toll (TL) = Marginal Cost = Demand (social marginal benefit) at V_2. By reducing demand from V_3 to V_2, this ensures the efficient use of road space, as inessential traffic switches to journeys at less crowded times (from D_1 off-peak to dotted D_2 off-peak). Nevertheless road tolls are often misunderstood and resented by motorists, as popular newspaper headlines indicate:

Daily Express, 9 June 2003

However, congestion, due to grow by 11–20 per cent by 2010, is forcing the UK government to seriously consider road pricing (for details see the news items on pages 101–102 and page 121). Apart from congestion externalities, other environmental consequences arising from noise, accidents, air pollution and the impact of road building must also be evaluated using cost–benefit analysis, explained in Chapter 6.

Government failure

So far we have identified environmental problems created by market failures. Can governments do any better? Disappointingly, government policies and activities, as a side-effect, can cause significant environmental damage:

- *In developed countries* there is sometimes conflict between environmental interests and government intervention to support farmers' incomes. The EU common agricultural policy, for example, intended to stabilize farm incomes and output, has increased the use of environmentally damaging pesticides and fertilizers. It has also encouraged the destruction of wildlife habitats such as small woodlands and hedgerows.

- *In developing countries* governments intervene with subsidies and controls – bringing prices below the market level – to assist the poor and promote economic development. These artificially low prices give the wrong signals, encouraging wasteful use of, for example, scarce energy and water resources. Although owned by governments, tropical rainforests are being destroyed, by concessions granted to commercial timber companies and peasant farmers, using the slash-and-burn method to clear land.
- *In command economies*, which replace markets by government controls, the record is even worse. The former Soviet Union, for example, now moving towards a market economy, is an environmentalist's nightmare. This is the legacy of the system which emphasized the achievement of planned output targets with little regard for consumers or the environment. Dissenting green views were suppressed. *Coase-style bargaining* between polluter and pollutees, to internalize environmental externalities, was unknown. Planners' targets ruled.

All of the problems noted above occur because governments fail to take account of the indirect environmental effects of their policies. Like market failures, government failures are also avoidable if corrective action is taken. This can be achieved by:

- ensuring that environmental standards are not overlooked by any government departments
- a systematic evaluation of all positive and negative externalities before starting any programme of government expenditure or legislation (see Chapter 6).

The latter provides a check on whether a proposed course of action is worthwhile – if the necessary social benefits exceed or are equal to social costs.

Summing up
The causes of environmental damage arise from a combination of related factors:

- externalities
- the lack of well-defined property rights
- the environment having characteristics of public goods.

These factors contribute to incomplete or missing markets. In turn these generate misleading prices, or no price at all, to guide producers and consumers towards socially efficient choices about the environment. To this list of causes we can add government failure.

However, many would assert that the major threat to the environment comes not from missing markets or from governments but from the pursuit of ever-increasing living standards or, less ambitiously, simply supporting an increasing world population. It is claimed that the higher output that this requires must involve the continuing destruction of natural resources. *Can we have economic growth and at the same time save the environment?* That is the theme of the next chapter.

KEY WORDS

Efficient pollution	Public goods
Abatement costs	Private goods
Marginal cost of abatement	Free-riders
Marginal social cost of pollution	Impure public goods
	Congestion externality
Missing markets	Government failure
Coase bargaining	

Further reading

Bamford, C., Chapter 6 in *Transport Economics,* 3rd edn, Heinemann Educational, 2001

Grant, S., and Vidler, C., Section 3.7 in Economics AS for AQA, Heinemann, 2003

Munday, S., Chapter 8 in *Markets and Market Failure*, Heinemann, 2000

Nixon, F., Chapter 6 in *Development Economics*, 2nd edn, Heinemann, 2001

Useful websites

DETR on roads: www.roads.detr.gov.uk/roadnetwork/heta/sactra98.htm
US Environmental Protection Agency: www.epa.gov/

Essay topics

1. (a) What are the social costs and benefits involved in the use of private cars? [10 marks]
   (b) Discuss whether government intervention designed to reduce traffic congestion will always improve the situation. [15 marks]
2. (a) Distinguish between a private and a public good. [10 marks]
   (b) Discuss whether the following are private or public goods: (i) defence, (ii) education, (iii) air purity, (iv) roads. [15 marks]

Data response question

This task is based on a question set by Edexcel in 2002. Study the extract and figure and then answer the questions that follow.

Extract

Market forces and the environment

Governments everywhere have tended to follow a heavy-handed 'regulatory' approach to environmental matters that sets ambitious goals and involves needlessly expensive responses or rigid technological requirements. Despite some notable successes, the resulting policies have encouraged legal disputes and discouraged innovation. The (5) regulatory approach has not proved all that effective. Although air and water quality have indeed improved dramatically, other environmental problems — from waste management to hazardous releases to fisheries depletion — have not.

Moreover, these government controls are inefficient, meaning that (10) even the gains that the world has seen have come at an unnecessarily high price. There has been little consideration for local environmental conditions or for the marginal cost of pollution reduction at individual companies.

Slowly but surely, governments around the world are rethinking the (15) regulatory approach. Instead they are experimenting with various types of market-based policies that could harness the power of the market to reduce external costs.

Market-based solutions differ from the regulatory sort in that they try to influence behaviour by altering price signals, rather than through (20) regulations. The regulatory approach gives companies very little choice in how they meet pollution targets. That means they cannot respond to local differences, and will continue to use old technologies and stifle innovation.

Robert Stavins, an environmental economist at Harvard University, (25) argues that the market mechanism does precisely the opposite. There are many types of market-based instruments available. He has divided them into four broad categories: tradeable permit schemes; green taxes and charges; the reduction of environmentally harmful subsidies (for example coal mining); and the removal of barriers to the creation of new (30) markets.

Some economists argue that such measures do not go far enough. What they want is a dramatic shift to a policy grounded in private property rights. Free-market environmentalists argue that the incentives and markets created by such rights will protect the environment better than (35) any amount of intervention that can lead to government failure. The absence of property rights often leads to users over-exploiting otherwise renewable resources. This is what has happened to offshore fisheries. Most of the world's fishing grounds are greatly depleted by over-fishing.

Figure Effects in 2020 of removing environmentally harmful subsidies, applying a carbon tax on fuels and a chemical-use tax in OECD countries, 1995 = 100

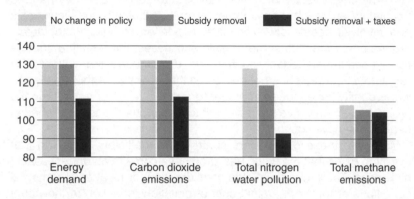

Source: The Economist Newspaper Limited, London 29 September 2001

1. (a) Distinguish between private costs and external costs. [4 marks]
   (b) Using an appropriate diagram, analyse the difference between the free market level of output and the socially efficient level of output for a pollution generating activity. [6 marks]
2. (a) Explain what is meant by 'government failure' (line 36) [2 marks]
   (b) Examine the view that 'the regulatory approach has not proved all that effective' in dealing with environmental issues (lines 5–6). [10 marks]
3. Evaluate the likely effectiveness of any two of the 'market-based instruments' for environmental improvements referred to in line 27). [12 marks]
   [Q1, Edexcel, Unit 2, May 2002]

Chapter Four
Sustainable development

'The world provides enough to satisfy every person's need, but not every person's greed. Mahatma Gandhi

The issues
A growing world population and rising expectations amongst the rich and poor will cause the output of goods and services to increase significantly for the foreseeable future. Whether or not the environment will be able to support this increase in the longer term, without suffering irreparable damage, is the question that lies at the heart of sustainable development. Two likely consequences of rising living standards will be the eventual exhaustion of many of the world's natural resources and the inability of the environment to absorb increasing amounts of waste.

This threat has given rise to different views about the relationship between increases in GDP and the environment. Some writers, such as Meadows, have argued that it is this very increase in goods and services which damages the environment and should therefore be curbed. The extreme version of this approach calls for zero growth. The opposite view is that slower or zero growth would deprive society of the very resources that it needs to deal with environmental problems. Proponents of this view, such as Beckerman, point to the fact that it is the wealthy countries of the world that have taken the lead in cleaning up the environment.

The Environmental Kuznets Curve
A systematic relationship has been claimed by some economists to exist between economic growth and the environment. Known since the early 1900s as the Environmental Kuznets Curve (EKC), this relationship casts doubt on the widely accepted belief that it was the wealthier countries with their high rates of consumption that most damaged the environment. In fact EKCs showed that some key indicators of environmental quality, such as air pollution, began to improve as incomes and consumption increased. The existence of EKCs has important policy implications because it suggests that some environmental damage is unavoidable as a country proceeds along its

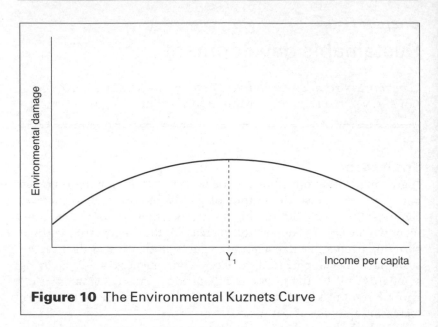

Figure 10 The Environmental Kuznets Curve

development path, especially in the early phase of industrialization. It also implies that when a certain level of per capita income has been achieved continued economic growth helps to repair the damage inflicted in earlier years.

Figure 10 shows that as per capita income rises environmental damage also rises until it reaches a maximum when incomes are at Y_1. After this point incomes continue to grow but environmental quality begins to improve.

Evidence is beginning to emerge, however, that supports the view that EKCs may only exist at the local level. For example, a particular polluting activity might be opposed by local residents who have sufficient incomes to conduct a successful campaign against it. At the national or global level it seems as if environmental impacts, such as traffic volumes, energy use and waste production, continue to rise as incomes rise and that there is, in fact, no upper limit.

Even if they did exist EKCs would not be enough on their own to bring about change because environmental improvement depends ultimately on policies and institutions. Growth in GDP creates opportunities for environmental improvement by raising the demand for a better environment and by making the resources available for achieving it. Whether the improvements actually materialize or not

> The UK's economy has grown by nearly 17 per cent since 1997 and in that time emissions have fallen by 5 per cent. The picture on resource use is also encouraging. Recent European research showed that the UK's total resources requirements grew by just 13 per cent between 1970 and 1999, whilst our GDP increased by 93 per cent. We in Britain have shown that it is possible to break the relationship between economic growth and ever-rising pollution.
>
> Source: Tony Blair, Prime Minister, 24 February 2003

depends largely on government policies, social institutions, and market efficiency.

The origins of sustainable development

The concept of **sustainable development** was first introduced by the forestry industry almost a century ago. It re-emerged as a key issue in environmental economics in the 1980s in response to growing concerns about the long-term availability of natural resources. It was put firmly on the international agenda in 1987 by the United Nations when it published the influential report of the World Commission on Environment and Development. Popularly known as the Bruntland Report (after its chairperson, Mrs G H Bruntland, prime minister of Norway) *Our Common Future* emphasized:

- Meeting the essential needs of the world's poor – jobs, food, energy, water and sanitation
- Integration of economics and the environment in decision making at all levels
- Promotion and improvement in the quality of development, and the conservation and enhancement of the resource base
- Effective citizen participation in decision making
- Sustainable population levels
- An international economic system that encourages sustainable patterns of trade and development.

Defining sustainable development

Because the concept means different things to different people and involves a range of value judgements, defining sustainable development is not easy. Pearce, for example, in *Blueprint for a Green Economy* was able to list 24 different definitions. Perhaps the most widely accepted definition is the one given in the *Bruntland Report* which defines it as '...*development that meets the needs of the present generation without compromising the ability of future generations to meet their own needs.'* An analysis of some of the words in this statement provides some clear insights into the debate about sustainable development.

'Development'

Increases in real per capita GDP, although important in people's lives, are not the same as development. The United Nations Development Programme (UNDP) measures development by reference to its human development index (HDI). This is based on the following four variables:

- Life expectancy
- Adult literacy
- Educational enrolments
- Per capita GDP.

The basic goal of development therefore is to create the circumstances that enable people to live long, healthy and creative lives.

Income, economic growth and human development

Income is a means to human development but it is not the only one. Through various means the benefits of an increasing income need to be translated into enhancing different aspects of human well being. Economic growth is a necessary, but not sufficient, condition for human development. It is the quality of growth, not just its quantity, which is important in people's lives. As the 1996 Human Development Report pointed out, growth can be jobless rather than job creating, ruthless rather than poverty reducing, voiceless rather than participatory; rootless rather than culturally enshrined; and futureless rather than environmentally friendly. Economic growth which is jobless, ruthless, voiceless, rootless and futureless is not conducive to human development.

Source: United Nations Development Programme

'Needs'

Unlike demand, which is the willingness and ability to buy goods and services at specified prices, 'needs' imply an ethical approach to what might be called essential community and individual requirements. What a need is will therefore vary over time and between places so a precise definition is virtually impossible. The *Bruntland Report* recognized this difficulty when it distinguished between essential needs and perceived needs which it saw as being socially and culturally determined. It warned that the satisfaction of perceived needs today may be at the cost of future generations satisfying their essential needs.

'Present and future generations'

The idea of fairness or equity permeates the entire discussion of sustainable development and it has two forms: **intra-generational equity** (within generations) and **inter-generational equity** (between generations).

The significance of intra-generational equity for environmental issues lies in the fact that it is the world's poor, in rich and poor countries alike, who suffer most from environmental degradation. These people also make the least demands on environmental resources. Furthermore, it is the poorest of the world who rely most heavily on such natural assets as fuel wood; vegetation for human consumption, clothing and shelter; wild animals and fish for protein; and on untreated water supplies. The more these resources are depleted and degraded the more people in poorer countries will come to depend on technological substitutes and the greater will be the responsibility of the developed world to make this technology available.

The contrast between rich and poor countries is illustrated in the following statistics:

- The USA has 5 per cent of the world's population. It uses 25 per cent of the world's energy and accounts for 22 per cent of all carbon dioxide emissions.
- India has 16 per cent of the world's population. It uses 3 per cent of the world's energy and accounts for 3 per cent of all carbon dioxide emissions.
- The USA produces 25 per cent of world GNP (at market exchange rates) whereas India produces just 1 per cent.

The question of inter-generational equity arises because the present generation derives benefits from using the environment as a source of amenity, a waste sink and a resource base but the costs of such use are passed on to future generations. The most obvious example is the nuclear energy industry which is producing radioactive waste that will remain hazardous for thousands of years.

There are two broad views about how this time separation of costs and benefits can be dealt with.

- The first requires that future generations are protected only from catastrophe, into which category fall global warming and ozone depletion. There the responsibility would end, and the resource depletion, species extinction etc. would be tolerated for the benefit of the present generation, whilst future generations would have to make do with whatever they inherited.
- The second more demanding interpretation requires that future generations are enabled to enjoy the same levels of environmental consumption as the present generation. However, there are difficulties involved in specifying exactly what should be inherited (the **stock of assets**).

CHERNOBYL'S legacy could continue to blight Welsh sheep farming for years to come, it was revealed yesterday. The threat comes from proposed enlargement of the European Union that could lead to even tighter rules that apply to some 180,000 animals that have radioactive traces. One of the many farmers who would be affected after years of coping with existing restrictions is Glyn Roberts of Padog, near Betws-y-Coed, Conwy.

Mr Roberts's farm was placed under restrictions after the Chernobyl disaster in 1986 and he had no idea the same rules would still bind him 17 years later. 'They told me the restrictions would last six weeks,' he said yesterday. Mr Roberts's is not a one-off case where the radiation stubbornly refuses to go away because of some freak of geography or climate. Figures from the Food Standards Agency show that this month 360 farms in North Wales are still struggling with the additional bureaucracy of the Chernobyl restrictions.

Western Mail, 18 March 2003

The stock of assets

As we saw earlier, the Bruntland Report stated that sustainable development means that the present generation should not deprive later generations of the resources needed to satisfy their needs. In practice this means that they should inherit a stock of assets no smaller than the one inherited by the present generation. The stock of assets comprises the following:

Natural capital (renewable and non-renewable) +
manufactured capital + human capital (skills and knowledge).

Clearly this stock of assets cannot be passed on unchanged because, in the case of exhaustible resources, depletion is a consequence of use. In this case the issue becomes one of substitutability between natural and man-made assets. For example, some would argue that the

Table 3 Environmental viewpoints

Colour	Environmental position
Brown	• All assets are substitutable. • Technocentric view – benefits of knowledge and technology embodied in manufacture capital can outweigh the loss of natural capital. • Technical fixes can solve environmental problems. • Free markets are the best way of ensuring efficient use of resources. • Growth not a problem.
Light Green	• Some substitution between natural and manufactured capital is possible but is subject to the need to preserve essential natural resources – critical natural capital – in order to avoid irreversible environmental damage. • Markets adjusted for market failure – green prices and standards. • GDP growth constrained by the need to preserve a constant capital stock.
Deep Green	• Substitution undesirable. • Ecocentric view: virtually all ecosystems should be preserved. • Very deep green bio-ethical attitude: nature is sacred – all environmental assets (animate and inanimate) have moral importance. • Need for steady state economy, zero GDP and population growth. • Strong regulation rather than market forces to achieve environmental objectives.

complete exhaustion of fossil fuels and their replacement by solar energy technology is consistent with sustainable development.

For renewable resources, such as forests, sustainability could mean a constant physical stock or, alternatively, a constant economic value which would allow for a declining physical stock as prices rise. The composition of the asset base could also change by substituting man-made for natural capital but its productive capacity would remain unchanged.

There is a range of views (Table 3) about such substitutability and more generally about the trade off between the environment and new houses, roads, airports, tourist developments, etc. Broadly speaking, however, a distinction can be made between the anthropocentric approach, which puts humankind at the centre of the debate and sees the environment simply as a means of satisfying its wants, and the ecocentric approach, which claims that all life forms have a valid claim to existence irrespective of human wants.

Bio-diversity

Conserving bio-diversity – the variety in all life forms – is also essential for the maintenance of a good quality stock of natural assets. It is the destruction of habitats such as tropical forests, rather than over-exploitation, which is the main cause of the probable loss of one million species in the last twenty years, out of an estimated total of perhaps thirty million species. The case for bio-diversity is threefold:

- Wild species of plants and other life forms supply a significant amount of bio-chemical information from which modern medicines are developed. Approximately one quarter of prescribed medicines originate from plants. The familiar aspirin, for example, is based on a derivative of willow bark. Wild plants also provide material for breeding sturdier agricultural crops. Since future needs cannot be anticipated, a strong claim can be made for the greatest possible bio-diversity.

- The more abundant the bio-diversity, the greater the ability of the environment to withstand stress and shocks, such as floods, persistent droughts or viral outbreaks. With a diverse genetic stock, there is a greater possibility of adaptation and the survival of environmental systems.

- Irrespective of its practical value, the diversity of life is important for the enrichment of human experience, as a source of wonderment, contemplation and questioning.

Maintaining bio-diversity is not without cost. It may be impossible to preserve all species and have development, but as the environmental economist Pearce has concluded: 'We should only degrade or deplete our natural capital stock – particularly resources that may be irreversibly lost – if the benefits of doing so are very large.' Such important decisions require cost-benefit analysis, which is the systematic comparison of all costs and benefits, including externalities, extending into the future (see chapter 6).

International policy on sustainable development

The most significant event in the recent history of sustainable development was the United Nations conference on Environment and Development – the Earth Summit – held in Rio de Janeiro in 1992. At this gathering world leaders committed themselves to the principles of sustainable development when they agreed to Agenda 21, an environmental action plan for the twenty-first century. They also signed treaties on climate change and bio-diversity and agreed a statement of principles on forestry. At the same time the Commission on Sustainable Development (CSD) was created to ensure effective follow-up of the Rio commitments and to monitor and report on implementation of the agreements at the local, national, regional and international levels.

THE RIO DECLARATION

This declaration, about balancing the need to protect our environment with the need for development, is based on the following principles:

- The importance of sustainable development because we are concerned for people's quality of life
- The sovereignty of states and their responsibility not to cause environmental damage beyond their borders
- The importance of development so as to meet the needs of present and future generations
- The importance of tackling poverty, one of the root causes of environmental degradation
- Reduction and elimination of unsustainable patterns of production and consumption
- Public participation in decision-making and access to information
- Preventive measures to protect the environment in the absence of full scientific certainty (the preventive principle)
- Application of 'the polluter pays' principle by including environmental costs in the prices of goods and services
- Assessing the environmental impact of major projects.

The most recent initiative in the drive towards sustainable development was the World Summit on Sustainable Development held at Johannesburg in 2002. There was widespread agreement at this meeting that progress in implementing sustainable development had been extremely disappointing since the 1992 Earth Summit, with poverty deepening and environmental degradation worsening.

Johannesburg did not produce a particularly dramatic outcome but some important new targets were established. These included:

- halving the proportion of people without access to basic sanitation by 2015
- using and producing chemicals by 2020 in ways that do not lead to significant adverse effects on human health and the environment
- maintaining or restoring depleted fish stocks to levels that can produce the maximum sustainable yield on an urgent basis and where possible by 2015
- achieving by 2010 a significant reduction in the current rate of loss of biological diversity.

British policy on sustainable development

In the UK the concept of sustainable development was popularized by the publication of *Blueprint for a Green Economy* (the Pearce Report) which was originally prepared as advice for the Department of the Environment. Pearce's views were reflected in the British government's first major statement on the environment, *This Common Inheritance*, published in 1990.

'Sustainable development should be the organizing principle of all democratic societies, underpinning all other goals, policies and processes. It provides a framework for integrating economic, social and environmental concern over time, not through crude trade-offs, but through the pursuit of mutually reinforcing benefits. It promotes good governance, healthy living, innovation, life-long learning and all forms of economic growth which secure the natural capital upon which we depend. It reinforces social harmony and seeks to secure each individual's prospects of leading a fulfilling life.'

Source: Jonathan Porritt, Chairman, Sustainable Development Commission

---

By 1994 the UK had become one of the first countries to produce a sustainable development strategy in response to the call made at Rio, when it published *Sustainable Development: The UK Strategy*.

Subsequently, in an attempt to integrate the environment, social progress and the economy into the heart of policy making, the government published *A better quality of life: A strategy for sustainable development for the UK* in 1999. This identified the following four main aims:

- social progress which recognizes the needs of everyone
- effective protection of the environment
- prudent use of natural resources

- maintenance of high and stable levels of economic growth and employment.

The Sustainable Development Commission, an independent advisory body, with twenty-two members drawn from business, NGOs, local and regional government and academia, was established in 2000 to monitor this commitment.

Concluding comment

At the core of the idea of sustainable development is the role of the present generation acting as a custodian for a stock of assets which is to be passed on to future generations. As Lester Brown has commented in his book *Building a Sustainable Future*:

'We have not inherited the Earth from our fathers, we are borrowing it from our children.'

To help us decide what to preserve and enhance, we need to develop ways of valuing such natural assets as the atmosphere and the oceans which are not normally priced in the marketplace. Crucial to this process will be the creation of a new system of national accounts to show the depreciation of natural assets. These and other issues of environmental evaluation are considered in the next chapter.

KEY WORDS

Sustainable development   Intra-generational equity
Economic growth   Inter-generational equity
Environmental Kuznets Curve   Stock of assets
Development

Further reading

Bamford, C., Chapter 7 in *Transport Economics*, 3rd edn, Heinemann, 2001

Common, M., Chapter 9 in *Environmental and Resource Economics*, 2nd edn, Longman, 1996

Grant, S., and Vidler, C., Section 3.8 in Economics AS for AQA, Heinemann, 2003

The UK's Strategy for Sustainable Development, HMSO, 1994

Useful website

UN Commission on Sustainable Development:
www.un.org/esa/sustdev/

Essay topics

1. (a) Explain what is meant by sustainable development. [10 marks]
   (b) Discuss how sustainable development could be achieved. [15 marks]
2. Discuss whether a country should aim for high growth. [25 marks]

Data response question

This task is based on a question in an AQA paper in 2003. Study the extracts and then answer the questions.

Extract A

Biggest overall consumers of energy (measured in millions of tonnes of oil equivalent, 1998)

Rank	Country	Energy consumption
1	United States	2182
2	China	1031
3	Russia	582
4	Japan	510
5	India	476
6	Germany	345
7	France	256
8	Canada	234
9	United Kingdom	233
10	Brazil	175

The most efficient users of energy (energy intensity, 1998)

Rank	Country	Energy intensity figure
I	Switzerland	0.11
2	Denmark	0.13
3	Italy	0.14
4	Austria, Japan	0.15
5	Hong Kong, Ireland, Norway	0.16
6	Germany	0.18
7	France, Spain	0.19
8	Luxembourg, Netherlands, Sweden, United Kingdom	0.21
9	Finland, Gabon	0.22
10	Israel	0.24

(The USA is joint 16 with Panama, at a figure of 0.31)

Source: by permission of *The Reader's Digest Association Limited, Facts at Your Fingertips* © *2001.*

Extract B
International energy consumption

'Energy equivalence' calculates the use of all forms of energy, including all fossil fuels and other resources such as nuclear, hydroelectric, geothermal, wind and solar power, and gives a total in terms of the equivalent amount of oil. The world's most developed economies are its largest consumers of energy. Every year, the USA consumes energy in (5) all its forms equivalent to around 8 tonnes of oil per head of population; its poorer neighbour Mexico consumes just 1.5 tonnes per head. The world as a whole currently consumes energy equivalent to 9.5 billion tonnes of oil per year, an average of more than 1.6 tonnes for each person.

Most of this energy is created by burning non-renewable resources (10) such as oil and coal. How long these will last depends on the speed of industrialisation in less developed countries, and on global efforts to conserve energy by using it more efficiently. Fossil fuels are currently used to produce more than 80% of the world's energy. Eventually they will run out and renewable resources will have to replace them. (15)

The energy efficiency of a country can be measured by calculating how much energy it uses to produce each unit of its gross domestic product (GDP). Dividing a country's annual energy consumption (in tonnes of oil equivalent) by its GDP (in thousands of US dollars) produces an 'energy intensity' figure. The lower the figure, the more efficiently the country uses (20) energy. Various factors affect efficiency, including conservation measures such as building insulation, the balance between different forms of transport, and the ratio of manufacturing to services in creating GDP.

Source: by permission of *The Reader's Digest Association Limited, Facts at Your Fingertips* © 2001.

1. What is meant by the term 'gross domestic product' (Extract B, line 17)? [4 marks]
2. Explain why energy efficiency is important for protecting the environment. [6 marks]
3. Is the energy consumption of richer countries more likely to harm the environment than that of poorer countries? Use the data to help justify your answer. [10 marks]
4. Many consumer goods depend on oil-based fuel for transport to markets, or use oil as a raw material in production. With the help of a supply and demand diagram, analyse the possible long term effects on consumer prices of our dependence on oil. [10 marks]
5. Identify and evaluate policies that governments could use to encourage energy efficiency. [20 marks]
   [Q2, AQA, Unit 3, January 2003]

Chapter Five

How much for the environment?

'An economist is a person who knows the price of everything and the value of nothing.' Adapted from Oscar Wilde

Introduction

This chapter looks at two related questions which must be faced, in order to decide on the correct amount of resources needed to save and improve the environment:

- How much are natural assets and environmental quality worth?
- Can the environment be included in national accounts?

Valuing the environment

It is mistakenly thought that – as the quotation heading this chapter suggests – economists have a narrow view of life, being interested only in 'market prices'. In fact, establishing ways of valuing environmental goods for which markets are absent or incomplete is an important concern of modern economics. The following section briefly reviews the scope and limitations of the various techniques currently in use.

Physical damage valuation

If the physical effects of pollution are measurable – for example, damage to health, crops or buildings due to air pollution – then the costs of these impacts and the value of avoiding them might be calculated. In the case of health these costs would include medical bills and the value of output lost due to illness. Although useful, the technique has limitations. It ignores, in the case of health, the distress of illness and has an unacceptably restricted approach to the value of fitness and the quality of life. It is of no help in cases of environmental damage where the physical effects, such as loss of landscape or species, cannot be translated into costs using market prices.

Willingness to pay

An alternative to concentrating on the cost of damage is to find out how much people are willing to pay for environmental improvement or preservation. There are two ways of doing this:

1. Revealed preference

This is known as **revealed preference** because, even where markets for environmental goods do not exist, consumers may indirectly reveal how much they value them, through other actions or expenditures. For instance, demand curves for the enjoyment of the countryside might be constructed from the travel times and costs people incur to reach their destinations, which can be regarded as a price paid for access to the countryside.

The demand for clean air and quietness has been inferred from comparisons of the prices of similar houses in areas differing in noise levels or air pollution. On a house costing £50 000, for example, various studies estimate that in certain areas a 10 per cent decrease in air sulphur pollution might raise the price by £600 and a one-decibel decrease in traffic noise by £250.

2. Stated preference

Typically this group of techniques (**stated preference**) involves the use of carefully worded questionnaires to find out people's **willingness to pay** (WTP) for environmental improvement, or **willingness to accept** (WTA) compensation for an equivalent deterioration in the quality or quantity of environmental assets. Illustrations, models and videos may be used to help make the questionnaire more realistic.

In its most simple form a WTP question might ask: 'How much are you willing to contribute to save a public woodland near your home?' It might be expected that, for a particular environmental good, the value at which people are willing to buy (WTP) would be equal to the value at which they are willing to sell (WTA). Disconcertingly, WTA values are usually significantly higher. No single, totally persuasive explanation has been found. Among possible explanations is the difficulty of replacing environmental goods with other goods. Stereos and mountain bikes, for example, are probably inadequate substitutes for the loss of woodlands. Higher compensation is required for the environmental loss.

A feature of some stated-preference techniques is the use of experimental designs, to construct a series of hypothetical alternatives from which individuals are then asked to choose. Instead of the question 'How much are you willing to contribute to saving the elephant?', respondents might be asked to rank, in order of preference, alternative wildlife programmes for a given cost, with different levels of preservation in the numbers of elephants, rhinos and mountain gorillas.

This technique can be extended to include manufactured as well as environmental assets. For example, in determining priorities for a development plan a local government council may have to consider:

- providing more industrial jobs
- preventing the loss of open land
- providing new housing
- conservation of wildlife
- promoting tourism in the area.

Data would be presented in the questionnaire, on the opportunity cost of, for example, extra houses or jobs in terms of the loss of open land or wildlife. Residents would then be asked to rank alternative development plans. This technique therefore provides information on peoples' marginal rates of substitution or trade-off between different goods or qualities of goods. If monetary costs can be put on one of the goods in the survey, then WTP can be estimated.

An obvious difficulty is that all the stated-preference methods rely on answers to hypothetical questions and may be subject to certain biases because respondents are not making real transactions.

'Hello! We can't be far from civilization'

Source: Punch Cartoon Library

Total economic value (TEV)

People may be ready to pay for environmental assets they never experience directly. Contributions to saving the panda, for example, or other threatened species, may come from people who never expect to see the creatures in the wild except in television programmes or photographs.

- **Use value** is what people are willing to pay to use the environment – for recreation; as a source of agricultural land and materials; as a receptacle for waste.
- **Option value** is the amount people are prepared to pay in order to

preserve the option to use some environmental asset at a later date. Even if the option is not exercised, the possibility of doing so may be a source of satisfaction.

- **Existence value** is what people will pay for the satisfaction of knowing that a species or habitat exists, although they will never visit or use it. Preserving the environment for one's heirs and for future generations, as well as a belief in the 'sanctity of nature', are among the sources of existence value.

Total economic value =
use value + option value + existence value.

National accounts

A precondition for the management of environmental resources is a comprehensive system of measuring the stock and use of such resources.

We might expect that a likely source for such information would be the official national accounts which measure, for each country, wealth in terms of the total value of the flows of output, income and expenditure – the gross domestic product (GDP). In fact conventional GDP accounts are a very poor measure of human interaction with the environment. This is because GDP figures capture only market and other recorded transactions (on page 15, Figure 4; the upper loop in the diagram), whereas for the environment (on the lower part of the diagram), markets don't exist or are incomplete.

Specifically, GDP figures fail environmentally for the following three reasons:

- They don't show the depletion of natural resources. A country that runs down its stocks of machinery, by failing to replace them as they wear out, will be shown to be poorer, but a country depleting its fisheries or forests appears in GDP accounts to be richer.
- No account is shown of the value of environmental changes on the quality of life – variations in air and water purity; noise, pleasant views, access to countryside.
- Although the benefits of environmental improvements don't figure in national accounts, regrettable or 'defensive' environmental expenditures such as the £8 billion clear-up bill for the Exxon tanker oil spill, for example, may paradoxically show as an increase in GDP.

Why not simply produce an environmentally adjusted 'green GDP' figure, equivalent to *total economic value* described in the last section?

An invaluable environment

Statisticians are trying to adjust measures of national wealth for pollution and depleted resources. This turns out to be all but impossible.

The answer might be obvious: adjust national accounts to take account of changes in the environment. Statisticians have laboured for more than a decade to find a way to do this. In 1993 the United Nations, whose System of National Accounts provides a standardized basis for countries to record changes in their income, expenditure and wealth, published guidelines for 'satellite' – or separate – accounts that try to integrate environmental and economic measures. Many environmentalists want to go further and estimate a single measure of the effect of environmental damage on economic growth. This goal of constructing a 'green GDP' is an imaginative one. But increasingly, statisticians are concluding that it is unattainable.

Some assets, such as timber, may have a market value, but that value does not encompass the trees' role in harbouring rare beetles, say, or their sheer beauty. Methods for valuing such benefits are controversial. To get round these problems, the UN guidelines suggest measuring the cost of environmental damage. But some kinds of damage, such as extinction, are beyond costing, and others are hard to estimate.

Putting environmental concepts into economic terms raises other difficulties as well. Geography weighs differently: a tonne of sulphur dioxide emitted in a big city may cause more harm than the same tonne emitted in a rural area while a dollar's-worth of output counts the same wherever it is produced. And the exploitation of natural resources may not always have a cost. Is a country depleting resources if it mines a tonne of coal? All other things equal, the mining of that tonne might raise the value of the coal that remains in the ground, leaving the value of coal assets unchanged.

Some statisticians, such as Anne Harrison of the OECD, would like a compromise which at least tries to attach monetary values to the depletion of natural resources, while admitting that degradation may be almost impossible to capture. Statisticians, say this school, should continue to try to value whatever they reasonably can. But they may have to accept that degradation (such as the loss of clean air or nice views) cannot be included in national accounts.

Source: The Economist Newspaper Limited, London, 18 April 1998

Experts are divided on this issue. Some favour measuring environmental impacts in monetary terms. Others support physical measures, such as the amount of sulphur dioxide and other pollutants emitted by each sector of the economy. The article 'An invaluable environment' from *The Economist* reviews some of the problems with these differing views, but emphasizes that a single satisfactory green measure of GDP is unlikely. However, the attempt to include the environment in our accounts should not be abandoned. To have some environmental measures is better than having no measures at all.

This is particularly important for reaching correct decisions on specific projects if they are to be environmentally sustainable – enlarging a motorway, building a dam or out-of-town shopping mall, for example. Each of these requires a careful balancing of all costs and benefits including environmental and other externalities. This process – *cost–benefit analysis* – is the theme of the next chapter.

KEY WORDS

Revealed preference	Use value
Stated preference	Option value
Willingness to pay	Existence value
Willingness to accept	Total economic value

Further reading

Grant, S., Chapter 4 in *Economic Growth and Business Cycles*, Heinemann Educational, 1999

Grant, S., and Vidler, C., Section 3.8 in Economics AS for AQA, Heinemann, 2003

Grant, S., and Vidler, C., Section 3.3 in Economics AS for Edexcel, Heinemann, 2003

Perman, R., Common, M., McGilvray, J. and Ma, Y., Chapters 10 and 12 in *Natural Resources and Environmental Economics*, Longman, 1999

Useful website

Office for National Statistics: www.ons.gov.uk/ons

Essay topics

1. (a) Explain how the environment can be valued. [10 marks]
   (b) Discuss the problems involved in constructing a reliable measure. [15 marks]
2. Discuss whether the goods and services which create externalities should be necessarily provided by government. [25 marks]

Data response question

This task is based on a question in a 2002 paper from AQA. Read the extracts and then answer the questions.

Extract A

Not the end of the world

President George W. Bush has announced that the USA will abandon the international Kyoto protocol, which sought to reduce emissions of the greenhouse gases that are believed to cause global warming.

Here at home, Michael Meacher, the environment minister, described global warming as 'the most dangerous and fearful challenge to humanity over the next 100 years'. One of his Tory predecessors, John Gummer, spoke of waging a 'trade war' against the United States.

In reality, the world is not going to end as a result of Mr Bush's decision. Even if Kyoto proposals were rigorously adhered to, they would not affect the globe's temperature by more than a fraction of a degree over the next 50 years. The agreement's impact on American industry, on the other hand, would have been enormous.

Source: adapted from *The Daily Telegraph,* 30 March 2001

Extract B

Oh no, Kyoto

The Kyoto protocol was already in deep trouble before Mr Bush took office. At negotiations in The Hague in November 2000, the European Union (EU) refused to accept American arguments that targets could be met through more flexible mechanisms, including the claiming of credit for forests that absorb carbon dioxide (forest 'sinks'). (5

Only two EU members are reasonably close to their Kyoto targets — Britain, thanks to its 'dash to gas' in electricity generation; and Germany, thanks to the closure of much of East Germany's polluting industry. The rest of the EU is hardly more likely to meet the Kyoto targets than is America. If the Europeans maintain their hostility to market approaches (10 and continue their hypocritical attacks on Mr Bush, they could well cause negotiations to fail.

The US administration has given several arguments for opposing Kyoto. These include the lack of participation of poor countries and the economic burden imposed on the United States. (15

They argue that developing countries such as India and China are not required to cut emissions, and so get a 'free ride' from reduced externalities while America suffers economic hardship. The costs of the Kyoto protocol are not known precisely, often depending on value judgements rather than positive statements. However, most economists (20 agree that if the treaty is implemented with more flexibility to allow more use of market forces and encourage innovation and investment in clean technologies, the cost can be reduced. A number of experts agree that since global warming is caused by the growing stock of greenhouse gases in the atmosphere, rather than the flow of new gases, strict (25) controls in the short term make little sense. The cost of meeting a target can be substantially reduced by giving firms more time to adjust.

It is not only green groups that want action on climate change. Many of America's biggest businesses want the uncertainty surrounding future regulations ended. Those are the sorts of voices Mr Bush should heed. (30)

Source: The Economist Newspaper Limited, London, 7 April 2001

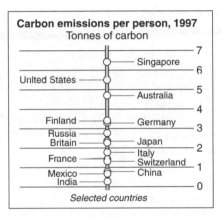

Carbon emissions per person, 1997
Tonnes of carbon
Selected countries

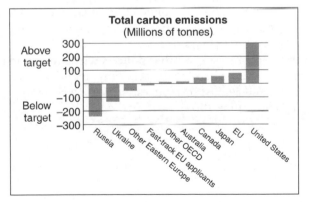

Total carbon emissions
(Millions of tonnes)

Extract C

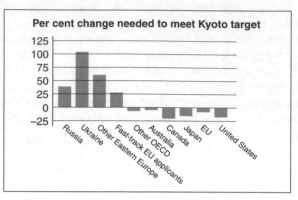

Per cent change needed to meet Kyoto target

Source: The Economist Newspaper Limited, London, 7 April 2001

1. (a) What is meant by the term 'externalities' (Extract B, line 18)? [4 marks]
   (b) Distinguish between 'value judgements' and 'positive statements' (Extract B, lines 19–20). [5 marks]
2. Do poorer countries get a 'free ride' (Extract B, line 17) while the USA suffers 'economic hardship' (Extract B, line 18)? Justify your answer using Extract C. [6 marks]
3. Explain why 'more flexibility' (Extract B, line 21) and 'giving firms more time' (Extract B, line 27) might be expected to reduce the cost of implementing emission targets. [7 marks]
4. With the help of an aggregate supply and aggregate demand (AS/AD) diagram, explain how the imposition of strict controls on the output of industries causing greenhouse emissions could affect output and inflation. [8 marks]
5. The extracts appear to suggest that policies which are good for the environment might be bad for the economy. Identify and evaluate arguments **for** and **against** this suggestion. [20 marks]
   [Q2, AQA, Unit 3, June 2002]

Chapter Six

Cost–benefit analysis

'... cost–benefit analysis is an imperfect calculus, as much an art as a science or, more precisely, as much a matter of judgement as technique.'
E. J. Mishan

Introduction
In an economy with a well-functioning market, resources are allocated to their most highly valued uses via prices which reflect their relative scarcity. However, in the case of natural resources and environmental goods these markets frequently do not exist or, if they do exist, are distorted or malfunction in various ways. This *market failure* has its origins in such elements as externalities, unpriced assets, public goods, transaction costs and non-existent property rights. The most significant consequence of this market failure is a divergence between social and private costs and benefits.

Cost–benefit analysis (CBA) was developed by public sector economists in order to identify and quantify the social costs and benefits of public sector investment projects. Subsequently CBA was used to evaluate policies as well as projects. Whether used to evaluate projects or policies, CBA is essentially a decision-making tool which assesses the allocation of particular resources according to a comparison of the wider costs and benefits. If a proposal indicates that benefits will exceed costs then it can be approved, and where there are several proposals they can be ranked according to size of the total net benefit.

The development of CBA
Although the first recorded use of CBA was in France in 1840 when a civil engineer, Jules Dupuit, used it to estimate the benefits of a bridge, modern-day CBA has its origins in the USA where the Flood Control Act of 1936 stipulated that flood control projects should only be undertaken if 'the benefits, to whomsoever they may accrue' exceed the costs. By the 1960s CBA was being used to evaluate many aspects of the federal budget, including military expenditure, and by the 1970s its use had been extended to environmental and energy issues.

Two of the earliest examples of the use of CBA in the UK are the evaluation of the M1 motorway in 1961 and the Victoria Line of the London Underground in 1963. A less well known example is the 1967 Department of Transport investigation into the Cambrian Coast railway line, but a significant one nevertheless because it represents an evaluation of disinvestment (i.e. closure) rather than investment. CBA was also used in 1970 by the Roskill Commission in its enquiry into the siting of a third London airport and by the Department of Energy in its 1981 and 1986 feasibility studies of a barrage across the Severn Estuary. For a recent example of CBA in the UK, see the 1996 investigation by the Home Office into road speed cameras (available at www.homeoffice.gov.uk/prgpubs/fprs20.pdf).

CBA procedure

In 1984, HM Treasury issued a set of guidelines to be used by government departments when undertaking investment appraisal exercises (CBA). The following procedure was suggested:

1. Define investment criteria
2. Identify options
3. Enumerate and calculate both direct and indirect costs and benefits of each option
4. Discount the monetary cost and benefits
5. Evaluate the risks and uncertainties
6. Consider the constraints
7. Present the conclusions indicating the preferred option and the basis of the calculation.

These guidelines represent a fairly standard approach to CBA and we can now discuss each in turn against the backdrop of current environmental concerns.

1. Define investment criteria

The most frequently cited investment criterion of CBA is the maximization of society's net benefit, and there are two classic positions on this topic.

Firstly, the **Pareto criterion** states that a net benefit exists when, following a change, at least one person is made better off without anyone being made worse off. Because of the very restrictive nature of this criterion – projects or policies involving income redistribution are clearly excluded – a second criterion known as the **Kaldor–Hicks criterion** is generally adopted. This approach, which forms the basis of current CBA, states that *a net benefit occurs when the sum of the benefits exceeds the sum of the costs, whether or not these benefits are* *used to compensate those who bear the costs.* That CBA does address the issue of gainers compensating losers is clearly a major source of criticism to which we shall return.

Another investment criterion used in CBA and widely referred to in the literature is the maximization of the **benefit-cost ratio** (BCR). This states that only those projects whose BCR ratio exceeds 1 should be adopted. Where there are several alternative projects they are ranked according to their BCR ratio and the project with the largest ratio is chosen. Unfortunately these competing criteria can often provide contradictory outcomes, as Table 4 shows.

Table 4 Comparison of net present value (NPV) and benefit–cost ratio (BCR)

Project	1. Present value of costs (£)	2. Present value of benefits (£)	Present value of net benefits (£) (2–1)	Benefit–cost ratio (2/1)
A	100	350	250	3.5
B	300	600	300	2.0
C	350	900	550	2.6

The table shows clearly that if the benefit–cost ratio criterion is used then project A is the preferred option, but if the present value of net benefits criterion is used then project C is the preferred option and project A becomes the least preferred option. Theoretically net present value is the most satisfactory criterion but it has been argued that other criteria should be included, particularly where a choice has to be made between a cluster of projects of various sizes with different NPVs. In this situation it is claimed that the BCR ratio is more appropriate.

Current research by the United Nations Development Programme has focused on attempts to formulate an approach to CBA which is consistent with sustainable development. What is emerging is the idea that in the foreseeable future, projects will be ranked not by their net present values but by the new concept of sustainable net benefit which includes many of the ideas covered in Chapter 4. Such a criterion would have obvious implications for current CBA procedures.

2. Identify options
For any given investment project there are likely to be several different options available. For example, the Department of Environment,

A5 bypass plans axed to spare Snowdonia

The Welsh Office controversially axed two massive A5 bypass plans yesterday, to protect the rural beauty of North Wales.

For the first time, the Snowdonia countryside was given precedence over the drive for faster motor traffic and the Bethesda and Llangollen bypasses were axed.

The announcement was cheered by environmental, wildlife and countryside groups which had campaigned for years against turning the A5 into a Euroroute.

Bethesda bypass would have torn its way through local woodland and the proposal to straighten the Padog Bends would have created a three-lane highway through 20 acres of National Trust land.

The Daily Post, 12 March 1997

Transport and the Regions (DETR) might have allocated funds to solve the traffic problems of an historic town where congestion is causing long delays, accidents to pedestrians, pollution and damage to buildings. Planners identify three possible routes for the bypass:

- a northern bypass
- a southern bypass
- realignment and widening of the existing road.

Additional options might include delaying or phasing-in any of the above, taking policy measures rather than spending decisions and simply doing nothing. In some instances doing nothing, with its own costs and benefits, is quite a sensible decision and makes more sense than proceeding with a project which wastes resources. Doing nothing also provides a benchmark which can be used to judge the real impact of a project.

3. Enumerate and calculate costs and benefits

The principal distinction between the selection of projects in the private sector and the public sector is that the former is primarily concerned with private costs and benefits and their impact on profits, whereas the public sector, with its concerns for the welfare of society as a whole, needs to take account of the wider social costs and benefits arising from any particular public investment. Of particular concern are the externalities generated by a project, whether these are positive or negative. It is only when these have been identified and quantified that total social cost and benefits can be calculated.

(i) Real and pecuniary costs and benefits

The first step in the enumeration of the social costs and benefits of any project is to distinguish between real and pecuniary costs and benefits. Real benefits are those benefits which are enjoyed by the consumers of the public project and as such reflect the increase in society's welfare. Real costs are the opportunity costs involved in withdrawing resources from other uses. For example, if we consider the bypass proposal mentioned earlier, we can identify the reduction in travel time and the reduction in accidents as real benefits which accrue to the motorists using the bypass. However difficult it may be to calculate these benefits, they quite clearly need to be included in any comprehensive appraisal of the bypass. In contrast, there may be other identifiable benefits which, because they are merely pecuniary, need to be excluded. Pecuniary benefits arising from the bypass would include the increase in the profits of those businesses, such as garages, pubs, cafes, etc., resulting from the diverted traffic. Since these gains would be offset by the losses incurred by similar businesses in the town itself there is no net gain to society. (Pecuniary benefits are similar to the transfer payments encountered in national income analysis.) In addition, to the extent that the increase in the profits of businesses located on the bypass is a reflection of the increase in traffic generated by the bypass, the benefits of which will have already been included as real benefits, their inclusion would involve double counting.

(ii) Direct and indirect costs and benefits

Another distinction which needs to be made is between direct (primary) and indirect (secondary) costs and benefits. In the case of our bypass example, the direct costs would include such items as the purchase of land and the cost of labour and materials used in its construction. Indirect costs might include the double glazing of nearby houses affected by the noise of the traffic using the bypass. The direct benefits of the bypass would include those mentioned earlier, such as reductions in journey times and accidents; whilst indirect benefits would include a less noisy and polluted town and possibly even a cappuccino at a pavement cafe!

(iii) Cost and benefit – tangible and intangible

Real costs and benefits can also be tangible or intangible. Given perfect markets, the tangible costs and benefits of a project can be measured by the prices of the goods or services involved. However, if market imperfections exist then market prices are not accurate reflections of the social valuation of these goods and services, and shadow or accounting prices need to be used to adjust for the distortion in market prices. Although this is a complication, it is not unduly problematic. Problems do arise when intangible costs and benefits have to be calculated. By definition they cannot be measured by using market prices since they do not exist and yet it is precisely these intangibles which are so important in CBA. For example, the construction of the bypass mentioned earlier would provide a reduction in journey times and accidents, but although they are very clearly benefits they are, nevertheless, intangible and some method of attaching a monetary value to them needs to be adopted.

> Taxes on motorists should be tripled to reflect the true cost of road transport, which adds £11 billion a year to health bills because of exhaust pollution, according to a report published by the British Lung Foundation in February 1998. Professor David Pearce, the author of the report, arrived at this figure by measuring the health effects and the willingness of people to pay to avoid the suffering caused by pollution.

(iv) Valuing time, noise and accidents
In valuing time a distinction needs to be made between working time and leisure time. The principle generally adopted in CBA for the valuation of working time is that one hour of working time saved is worth the hourly wage rate, whilst the valuation of leisure time is usually based upon the observed trade-offs which people make when confronted with the choice of a cheap but circuitous route and a more direct but expensive one. The monetary value of the reductions in accidents could be calculated by using existing DETR methodology, where the cost of road accidents is based upon the costs incurred by the NHS in treating road accident victims as well as the associated police and legal costs. The cost of the lost output of those injured should also be included. One estimate of the cost of road accidents is given in Table 5 (opposite).

Levels of noise in the environment would be significantly affected by the bypass. Lower noise levels in the bypassed town would be an obvious benefit to the townspeople, whilst people living adjacent to the new bypass would incur major costs because of the higher noise levels. The Eighteenth Report of the Royal Commission on Environmental Pollution – *Transport and the Environment* (Cm 2674), published in

Table 5 The cost of road accidents

Type of accident	Number of casualties	Cost per casualty	Total
Fatal	3 814	£744 060	£2.84 billion
Serious	45 009	£84 260	£3.79 billion
Slight	257 197	£6 540	£1.68 billion
			£8.31 billion

Source: Royal Commission on Environmental Pollution, *Eighteenth Report – Transport and the Environment*, Cm 2674, 1994

1994, identified road traffic as the most common and most pervasive source of noise in the environment and estimated its overall cost at between 0.25 per cent, and 1.0 per cent of GDP. At a more personal level, the 1996 White Paper *Transport: The Way Forward* (Cm 3234) suggested that on average an individual would value a decrease in noise of one decibel at between £5 and £10 per annum. (A decrease in noise of ten decibels (dB) is perceived as a halving of noise so that the noise level in a house, 60 dBs, with a window open on to a busy road would be twice the received level of noise, 50 dBs, if the window were closed.)

(v) Atmospheric pollution
The construction of the bypass would also have an effect on atmospheric pollution in the area. Although pollution in the town itself would be abated, it would increase in the immediate area of the bypass and these effects would need to be quantified. The 1996 White Paper suggests that on average an individual would value a reduction in particulates by one microgram per cubic metre at between £5 and £20 per annum. This is the context of average UK levels of 10–15 micrograms per cubic metre in rural areas and 20–30 micrograms in urban areas.

Consider also carbon dioxide (CO_2) which is the most significant of the greenhouse gases implicated in global warming (which has its own costs and benefits). In the UK, some 24 per cent of total CO_2 emissions come from surface transport of which 87 per cent originates from road transport. The 1996 White Paper used the average cost to world GDP each year of global warming, over the period to 2050, as the basis for estimating the cost of damage caused by CO_2 emissions. It estimated a cost of responsibility for UK transport at between £1.8 and £3.6 billion.

This discussion of CO_2 highlights the inside versus outside problem of CBA where a distinction needs to be made between benefits and costs which accrue inside the jurisdiction where the project is undertaken and those which occur outside. For example, in using CBA to evaluate the UK road-building programme just how much importance would be attached to the costs of increase in CO_2 levels? Should they be included at all? In practice it is extremely difficult to draw a geographical boundary within which all costs and benefits occur and beyond which they do not, but a decision has to be made nevertheless. Other intangibles would be the effect, positive or negative, which the construction of the bypass would have on the flora and fauna in the area. As we have seen already, such is the difficulty in quantifying these effects they are left out of the CBAs conducted by the DETR, but they are included in the environmental assessments to reflect growing public concern about the loss of habitat and the threat to bio-diversity.

(vi) Biased calculations

A problem which often emerges in CBA is **institutional capture**, where institutions and organizations use it for their own ends. For example, those who incur the costs of a project have a tendency to exaggerate them and to minimize the benefits, whilst those who have a vested interest in the project, such as construction companies (or environmental groups), can be expected to minimize the costs and

---

Some of the environmental degradation perpetrated by the Tennessee Valley Authority and others is carried out through the sophistry of cost–benefit analysis. One example was the US Army Corps of Engineers' $15.3 million Gillham Dam across the Cossatot River in Arkansas, which was halted by an Environmental Defense Fund sponsored injunction against the Corps. Three-quarters of the benefits claimed for Gillham Dam, $970 000 annually, were in flood damage that the Corps said the dam would prevent. Yet on the 50 miles of the flood plain below the dam there was virtually nothing to protect – in sum, three old wooden bridges, a dozen summer homes, and about 20 miles of gravel road. There had never been a recorded flood death on the Cossatot.

Upon inspection it appears that the figure of $970 000 was arrived at by the Corps through some circuitous reasoning. The dam was expected to result in a considerable growth in population and industry, which would mean that new buildings would be built on the present flood plain. It was the value of these anticipated structures that was being protected from flood by the dam. The only real beneficiaries of the dam, it turned out, were landowners who would reap a windfall profit as their forests were converted to industrial parks.

Source: D Thompson, *The Economics of Environmental Protection*, 1973

---

inflate the benefits. Although initially hostile to the whole concept of CBA, many environmentalists can now see the advantages of such an approach provided that the costs and benefits, about which they are so concerned, are included in the analysis.

4. Discount monetary costs and benefits

It is this stage in the CBA procedure which generates the most controversy among environmentalists and in order to understand the arguments involved we need to look at the rationale for a practice of discounting in some detail. In Chapter 4 we discussed the concept of *inter-temporal equity*, that is, fairness between generations. Comparing the value of money, resources or consumption over time, however, raises certain difficulties. The difficulties arise from the fact that most people have a preference for money or consumption today rather than at some time in the future. In other words they are attaching a different value to the same thing as it occurs over time. For example, if someone would prefer to have £100 now rather than the same £100 next year (which is usually the case), they are implicitly saying that the one £100 is more valuable than the other. There are three possible explanations for this:

- Firstly, people generally prefer to have things now rather than later, whether it is a sum of money, its equivalent in resources or even a good time! Economists describe this as pure time preference and apart from simple impatience – it has its source in the risk of death (people might not be alive at some time in the future) as well as uncertainty – who knows what the future might hold? For example, some catastrophe might occur to prevent the consumption of something which could have been consumed today. And people's preferences themselves may change over time so that what is forgone now for the sake of future consumption may not even be wanted in the future.
- Secondly, a sum of money received now could be invested and, at a positive rate of interest, would be worth more in, say, a year's time than the same amount of money received a year hence. For example, £1000 received and invested today at 5 per cent annual interest would, in a year's time, become £1050. By postponing the receipt of the £1000 for one year this opportunity to earn interest of £50 is lost. There is, in other words, an opportunity cost involved. This explanation is more commonly referred to as the capital productivity rationale for present consumption over future consumption.

• Thirdly, we would normally expect incomes and living standards to increase over time, but the theory of diminishing marginal utility tells us that the value of an extra slice of income is less than the preceding slice of income. Thus, as individuals see their incomes increase over time each pound spent in the future buys less utility. It is therefore worth less than a pound today which can buy more utility.

These are the explanations for **personal time preference** and in a market economy where consumer sovereignty prevails and individual preference determines the allocation of resources, the conventional view is that time preference should be considered alongside all other preferences in the economic decision-making process. Since a society is a collection of individuals, all of whom have time preference, society must also have a time preference. In this case we refer to **social time preference** which, whilst positive, is generally regarded as being less strong than personal time preference.

The process by which individuals or society explicitly recognize their time preference, by attaching a current value to a sum of money or environmental resource occurring in the future, is known as **discounting**. Its use in the past in cost–benefit analysis has been relatively uncontroversial, but its application to environmental impact assessments has been questioned by many environmentalists and even some economists (see the differing estimates in Table 6).

Table 6 Estimates of the environmental costs of road transport in Great Britain (£ billion per year at 1994 prices)

	Estimate 1	Estimate 2	Estimate 3
Air pollution	2.0–5.2	2.8–7.4	19.7
Climate change	1.5–3.1	0.4	0.1
Noise/vibration	1.0–4.6	0.6	2.6–3.1
Total environmental costs	4.6–12.9	3.8–8.4	22.4–22.9
Road accidents	5.4	4.5–7.5	2.9–9.4
Total social and environmental costs	10.0–18.3	8.3–15.9	25.3–32.3
Congestion costs	Not included	19.1	19.1
Total transport externalities	10.0–18.3	27.4–35.0	44.4–51.4

Source: Royal Commission on Environmental Pollution, *Twentieth Report – Transport and the Environment*, Cm 7752, 1996
Estimate 1: Royal Commission *Eighteenth Report*, 1994
Estimate 2: Newberry *Economic Journal 105*, 1995
Estimate 3: Maddison and Pearce *Blueprint 5: The True Cost of Road Transport*, 1996

Table 7 The effect of different discount rates

Income	Discounted at:		
	5%	10%	15%
£100 at end of year 1	£95.24	£90.90	£86.96
£100 at end of year 2	£90.70	£82.65	£75.76
£100 at end of year 3	£86.38	£75.19	£65.79
£100 at end of year 4	£82.27	£68.50	£57.14
£100 at end of year 5	£78.35	£62.11	£49.75
Total of present values	£432.94	£379.35	£335.40

Before we look at this controversy, however, let us spend just a little time doing some simple calculations.

The arithmetic of discounting

Discounting is simply the reverse of the more familiar process by which a sum of money invested at a positive rate of interest grows as it is carried into the future. For example, £82.19 invested at 4 per cent grows to £100 at the end of five years. Conversely, the present value of £100 to be received five years from today when discounted at 4 per cent is only £82.19 (see Table 7 above).

Two conclusions are clear from Table 7. Firstly, that for each **discount rate** the present value of a sum of money shrinks the further that sum is from the present. Secondly, that for any given year, the higher the discount rate the smaller the present value of any sum of money.

Discounting formula

The present value of any series of future sums can be found by using the formula:

$$PV = \frac{S_1}{(1+r)} + \frac{S_2}{(1+r)^2} + \frac{S_3}{(1+r)^3} \ldots \frac{S_n}{(1+r)^n}$$

where

PV is the present value,
r is the discount rate
$S_1 \ldots S_n$ are the future sums.

For example, suppose an income stream of £100 per annum for five years discounted at 8 per cent :

$$PV = \frac{200}{(1+0.08)} + \frac{200}{(1+0.08)^2} + \frac{200}{(1+0.08)^3} + \frac{200}{(1+0.08)^4} + \frac{200}{(1+0.08)^5}$$

71

$$= \frac{200}{1.08} + \frac{200}{1.17} + \frac{200}{1.26} + \frac{200}{1.36} + \frac{200}{1.47}$$

$$= 185.18 + 170.94 + 158.73 + 147.0 + 136.0$$

$$= £797.85$$

Thus the £1000 accumulated at the end of five years has a *present value* of £797.85.

Had we been discounting over 25 years the present value would have been less than 10 per cent of the nominal value, and over 50 years it would have been less than 1 per cent of the nominal value. Such is the impact of discounting, and we can begin to see why some environmentalists question its use, encouraging, as it does, present over future consumption.

The choice of discount rate

The foregoing discussion has explained the rationale for discounting but it hasn't told us what the discount rate should be. Should it reflect personal time preferences or social time preference? If we are to respect consumers' preferences regarding individual items of consumption then logically we should respect their preferences for present rather than future consumption. This reasoning suggests that the discount rate should be determined by personal time preference, but such a rate is difficult to establish in practice and could, in fact, be very high – as much as 26 per cent according to one estimate.

In contrast, it could be argued that since individuals underestimate the importance of future consumption and overestimate the importance of present consumption, the social rate of discount should be used. Furthermore, some would claim that individuals, as members of society, *should* care more about the future and be compelled to act accordingly by the adoption of the lower social rate of discount. In other words, future consumption should be treated as a merit good.

Among those who accept the need for discounting, the consensus is that it should be determined mainly by the *social opportunity cost of capital*. Thus the 8 per cent rate currently used by the National Audit Office in its evaluation of public sector investment reflects broadly the rate of return in the private sector. In the Roskill Commission report a rate of 10 per cent was used and significantly the rate used by the Forestry Commission is only 3 per cent which reflects, no doubt, concerns about the viability of an investment the returns on which are, typically, some 50 years in the future. The opportunity cost of capital also explains the 10

per cent discount rate used by the World Bank in deciding its len
programme to developing countries.

Some environmentalists have argued for zero or even negati
discount rates. A zero rate would mean that £1 today is worth £1 i
future, whilst a negative rate would value £1 in the future as worth more
than £1 today. The final section in this chapter will consider the
reasoning behind such arguments.

Discounting and the environment

Discounting has been criticized by many environmentalists and some
economists for several reasons:

Future generations

We saw earlier that one justification for discounting is that since future
generations are likely to be better off than the present generation, a given
sum of money in the future will, because of diminishing marginal utility,
have less value than today. However, whilst this may be true of money it
is doubtful if the same can be said of the environment. Although future
generations may be better off financially and materially, all the present
indications are that they will have less 'environment' in the future as a
consequence of resource depletion, pollution and loss of habitat and
species. If this turns out to be the case then future generations will, as the
theory of diminishing marginal utility goes into reverse, place a greater
value on the environment than the present generation. Hence the
argument for negative discount rates.

Time preference

The time preference justification for discounting, with its emphasis on
risk and uncertainty, has also been challenged on several grounds:

- The risk of individual mortality and its influence on inter-temporal
  choice cannot be used to justify society's inter-temporal choices
  because society is 'immortal' and is not, therefore, under the same
  pressure as the individual to consume now rather than later.
- Future preferences for a whole range of consumer goods may well be
  uncertain as tastes change and new products are developed but
  preferences for the life-sustaining environmental services such as
  energy, food and water are likely to remain constant and certain and
  their discounting cannot, therefore, be warranted on grounds of
  uncertainty.
- Even where uncertainty does exist it may be the result of something
  other than futurity, in which case discounting, especially using a
  single rate, is inappropriate.

73

uctivity of capital

productivity of capital argument in defence of discounting has been allenged by the environmental economist Jacobs, who asserts that ecause £100 invested today will grow at a compound rate, it is absurd to suppose that £100 worth of environment today will also grow at a compound rate. Jacobs says: '... biologists have yet to discover a relationship between interest rates and the expansion of the Earth's surface'. Discounting for him is a form of discrimination against future generations.

Present and future gains

Some critics have questioned not the use of discounting itself but rather the use of high discount rates on the grounds that it sacrifices the future environment for present gains. However, as the economist Pearce points out, this is not always the case. For example, although high discount rates may cause cost burdens to be passed on to future generations, those same discount rates, based on the social opportunity cost of capital, will discourage investment and slow down the very economic growth which causes so much harm to the environment. Similarly with natural resources, the demand for which varies inversely with the discount rate.

5. Evaluate the risks and uncertainties

Despite the growing sophistication of the measurement techniques used in CBA, decisions are, nevertheless, made in ignorance about the future. For example, assumptions have to be made about the physical quantities and qualities of inputs and outputs of the project; the future prices of these inputs and outputs; the life of the project; and the nature of consumer demand. Furthermore, predicting the environmental

Genetic food findings 'biased'

Leading consumer and environmental groups yesterday accused a House of Lords select committee on genetically modified foods of being biased, muddled and inaccurate after publication of a report that strongly backed the controversial technology. ...

The peers accepted in their report that there could be significant environmental risks in the technology but said that these were outweighed by substantial future economic benefits to farmers, the food industry and consumers. ...

The report was welcomed by the life-science industry but a Friends of the Earth spokesperson said the committee had been bamboozled.

The Guardian, 22 January 1999

consequences of projects creates additional uncertainty. T
widespread use of DDT in the 1950s created major short-term b
through the control of mosquitoes and crop pests, but its very har
long-term consequences for bird populations were not anticipatec
more recent example is the concern about the uncertaintr
surrounding the use of genetically modified crops (see above).

In CBA, *uncertainty* is not the same as *risk*. Where it is possible to
identify the probable outcome of a project the issue is one of risk, but
where such probabilities cannot be estimated the issue becomes one of
uncertainty. In other words, risk is measurable uncertainty, which
means that within CBA a risky outcome is more easily handled than an
uncertain one. Risk is incorporated into CBA by weighting each
possible outcome by the probability of its occurrence. Uncertainty is
rather more difficult to deal with and, although complex procedures
have been developed to respond to it, a commonsense approach is to
generate additional relevant information before decisions are made. If

---

The costs and benefits of controlling foot and mouth disease

Food and Farming Minister Lord Whitty announced on 23 January 2003
major changes to animal movements in England and Wales. The
announcement follows research commissioned by Defra after the
outbreak of foot and mouth disease in 2001. The research produced two
assessments. Firstly, a risk assessment of the impact of different control
regimes on the silent spread of the disease before it is known to be in the
country. Secondly, a cost benefit analysis of these different regimes which
compared the cost to the industry of restrictions on animal movements
and the overall benefits to the country resulting from disease control.

Defra had already commissioned a risk assessment of the probability
of disease reaching livestock either from illegal meat imports or from the
legal meat trade. Emerging results from this study were also assessed as
part of the decision.

Lord Whitty said the risk assessment and cost benefit studies had
tackled novel and complex problems in a relatively short timescale. 'While
the emerging findings did not provide unequivocal answers, the
Government has concluded that the best approach is to put in place a
standstill of six days provided that the industry demonstrated a
commitment to an effective programme of biosecurity controls and further
work to improve disease detection. The emerging results from the cost
benefit analysis do not provide a definitive conclusion on the optimum
length of the standstill but in most of the scenarios and on balance a six
day standstill appears appropriate.'

ɔt be demonstrated that some outcomes are more certain than , then there are no rational grounds for taking a decision. Indeed, any areas of environmental analysis further investigation into ıs of uncertainty has produced significant gains.

An alternative and less ambitious method of dealing with projects where little is known about the outcomes or their probabilities is to conduct a *sensitivity analysis*. For example, a CBA of a nuclear power station might be conducted by taking a variable, say the price of oil, and assuming the most pessimistic value, the most optimistic value and a range of values in between. Sensitivity analysis is also used to examine the impact on projects of variations in the discount rate. Thus, for any given project a discount rate of say 5 per cent might produce benefits greater than costs whilst a 10 per cent discount rate might produce costs greater than benefits.

6. Consider the constraints

Although the maximization of society's net benefit is the primary aim of CBA, it is important to recognize that there are likely to be various constraints which make this difficult or impossible to achieve – so forcing decision-makers to adopt a less than optimum solution. The most important of these constraints are:

- Technology constraints – the possible alternatives under consideration may be limited by the existing production function and technology. For example, nuclear fusion offers virtually unlimited supplies of energy without the dangerous radioactive

---

The environmental movement has tended to be deeply distrustful of the decision-making process, not least where CBA is practised, on the grounds that government departments and agencies are able to manipulate supposedly impartial procedures to get the results they want. For example a study of CBAs for land drainage schemes in the UK (often involving considerable ecological damage) identified sixteen techniques by which assessments were biased in favour of drainage. Appraisal of trunk roads using the joint CBA and environmental impact assessment framework do not appear to have had any effect on the volume of road building at all.

Source: M. Jacobs, *The Green Economy*, Pluto Press 1991

---

waste associated with nuclear fission. Unfortunately, billions of pounds spent on research, the technology doe exist to harness the energy created during nuclear fusion, so to work within existing technological constraints impos nuclear fission.

- Legal constraints – national and international law concerning se things as due process, planning procedures and property righ. would impose limits on a particular agency's activities. Thus Directive 85/337/EEC of the European Union introduced a system of environmental impact assessments to be used by member states in the prior evaluation of the possible effects of public and private projects on the environment.

- Administrative constraints – the successful implementation of a project requires that sufficient competent personnel be available to carry it through. If the skilled staff are not available then even the best conceived project with a very high net present value (NPV) is worthless.

- Distributional constraints – the costs and benefits of a project are usually distributed unevenly. For example, the benefits from one project may accrue to a low income group whilst those of another project may accrue to a high income group. If other things are equal

£400 000 cost of saving newts

Councillors are outraged that a campaign by activists to save protected newts has cost the local authority £400 000.

'At a time when we have limited budgets to spend on vulnerable elderly people, children and people with disabilities, I am shocked that we have been forced to spend this amount of money,' said the chairwoman of Flintshire's social services committee.

The council's arms-length disposal company, AD Waste, is moving from the nearly full Standard tip in Buckley to former Brookhill Quarry also near Buckley. If the move does not go ahead the council would have to spend

a lot of money transporting waste out of the county.

Greater crested newts – a legally protected species – were discovered in Brookhill and had to be moved to a specially built site for protection. But conservationists lodged a whole series of complaints, called the police and went to the European Commission, alleging that the council had not done the job properly.

Flintshire believes the extent of the works was far in excess of what was necessary to meet EU requirements. The authority says it was forced into the situation because it could have taken years to resolve in the courts.

The Daily Post, 3 February 1999

project may be preferred on distributional grounds. In
on, those groups who incur the costs associated with a project
variably not the same as those who enjoy the benefits. In the
e of the third airport for London, the Roskill Commission was
ticized for not considering the distributional implications of a
decision which would have created significant benefits for air
travellers, typically those on high incomes, while those on low
incomes would have borne the brunt of the costs in the form of
higher noise levels.
- Political constraints – a project with the highest NPV may not be
feasible because of the slowness of the political process. Public
enquiries into nuclear facilities and major road schemes are typical

---

A2 Bean to Cobham Widening Proposals

In March 2001 public consultation took place on three different route
options for widening the A2 to four lanes in each direction between
Bean and Cobham in Kent. After considering all of the responses
received, the transport minister announced that the Red Route had
been chosen as the preferred route.

The DETR Cost Benefit Analysis (COBA) model was used to assess
this scheme because it can accommodate larger highway networks.
COBA, as well as being the conventional tool for inter-urban highway
proposals, is also able to assess a network the size of the A2 highway
network without distorting the economic benefits.

The economic evaluation was based on a comparison of costs and
benefits with and without the proposed improvement scheme. The
costs included the capital cost of building the scheme, land cost,
supervision cost, preparation cost and also the delay cost incurred by
users during construction and maintenance periods. The benefits were
assessed by comparing travel time cost, vehicle operating cost,
accident cost and maintenance cost with and without the scheme. All
the costs and benefits were assessed for two assumptions about the
growth of the UK economy. One calculation was based on low
economic growth and a low traffic growth assumption, while the other
assumed high economic growth and high traffic growth.

Subject to the satisfactory completion of the statutory procedures,
construction could begin in 2005.

Source: The Highways Agency: www.highways.gov.uk

examples of this. Strong pressure groups can also pr
adoption of policies with the potential of large net bene
present government's attempt at restricting the use of the ,
motor car is a case in point.

- Budgetary constraints – frequently the largest of the options ur
  consideration offers the highest NPV, but because of the need
  work within a limited budget a smaller project with a lower NPV ha
  to be chosen.
- Ethical constraints – the notion, implicit in CBA, that monetary
  values can, and should be, attached to such things as wildlife, scenic
  views, peace and quiet and so on is rejected by many people on the
  grounds that they have intrinsic value which puts them beyond
  price. For CBA to influence decision-makers its assumptions and
  procedures need to be acceptable to the public.

7. Presentation of conclusions

Handled with care, cost–benefit analysis is potentially a rigorous and
systematic approach to the evaluation of alternatives, which has two
essential characteristics: consistency and explicitness. In presenting the
results of the analysis, the cost–benefit practitioner has to show that the
calculations and results are consistent with the stated assumptions and
objectives of the project. The procedures and methodologies need to be
explicitly stated together with any relevant constraints. If these
conditions are met then the conclusion of the analysis can be presented
to the decision-maker as follows: 'Given that your objective is the
maximization of net present value then, subject to certain specified
constraints, the preferred option to A is ...'

Concluding comment

The issues raised in this chapter have shown that there will be many
occasions when, on completion of a cost–benefit analysis of a large
project with significant and long-term environmental effects, there will
be sufficient reasons why intelligent and reasonable people will
disagree on the desirability of the project concerned. These are strong
grounds for rejecting the view that cost–benefit analysis is an economic
technique which can be mechanically applied to produce the correct
solution. They are also a reminder that used properly and sensitively,
CBA provides a framework within which society can analyse and
evaluate in a consistent fashion all the many economic and
environmental effects of public expenditure.

KEY WORDS

~eto criterion	Personal time preference
~aldor–Hicks criterion	Social time preference
~enefit–cost ratio	Discounting
Institutional capture	Discount rate

Further reading

Common, M., Chapter 8 in *Environmental and Resource Economics*, 2nd edn., Longman, 1996

Grant, S., and Vidler, C., Section 3.9, Economics AS for AQA, Heinemann, 2003

Hanley, N., and Splash, C., Chapters 5 and 6 in *Cost Benefit Analysis and the Environment*, Edward Elgar, 1993

Munday, S., Chapter 6 in *Markets and Market Failure*, Heinemann, 2000

Useful websites

The following web pages give some valuable insights into the cost–benefit techniques currently being developed by the Department of the Environment, Transport and the Regions:

www.roads.detr.gov.uk/roadnetwork/heta/hetacoba.htm
www.roads.detr.gov.uk/roadsafety/rvs/hen1_9.htm
www.roads.detr.gov.uk/roadnetwork/heta/sactra98.htm
www.roads.detr.gov.uk/itwp/appraisal/understanding/index.htm
www.roads.detr.gov.uk/itwp/paper/index.htm

The following web pages give a detailed account of the appraisal of police speed cameras:

www.homeoffice.gov.uk/prgpubs/fprs20.pdf

Essay topics

1. (a) Describe the major steps in a cost-benefit study. [10 marks]
   (b) Discuss the arguments for and against a special low or even zero rate of discount for environmental projects. [15 marks]
2. (a) Explain why cost-benefit analysis is often used by the government upon major new road schemes. [10 marks]
   (b) Discuss the difficulties involved in carrying out a cost-benefit analysis. [15 marks]

Data response question

The area depicted in the map below is a stretch of agricultur.
consisting mainly of grades 2 and 3, lying between towns A a
Agricultural land is graded on a 1 to 5 scale – grade 1 is 'exceptio.
fertile' and grade 5 is classified as 'wasteland'. To the north there is
area of grade 1 land – also a site of special scientific interest (SSSI). T
the west is a rapidly expanding industrial area heavily involved in the
export trade.

There is a growing population here, incomes are high, and many
people take frequent holidays on the coast and take the car ferry to
France for shopping expeditions. Large numbers of foreign tourists use
the A666 as they leave the ferry and head for the West Country.

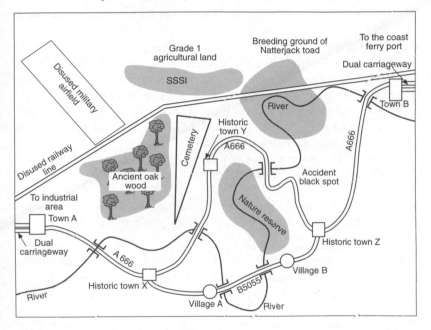

1. What are the transport problems in this area? [15 marks]
2. What environmental considerations would you need to take into account in dealing with these problems? [25 marks]
3. How would you overcome the transport problems? [20 marks]
4. What economic cost–benefit concepts and procedures would you use in your analysis of the problems and decision-making? [30 marks]
5. Draw a map of your preferred solution(s). [10 marks]

ıronmental improvement in theory:
∕vernment action

The primary virtue of the price mechanism is that it signals to consumers what the cost of producing a particular product is, and to producers what consumers' relative valuations are. In a nutshell this is the elegance and virtue of free markets which economists have found so attractive since the time of Adam Smith.'
D. Pearce, *Blueprint for a Green Economy*

Preliminaries
We have seen how environmental damage can be caused when markets do not work properly or because the necessary markets are missing. This and the following chapter review the theory underlying the repair work that can be carried out using the economist's toolkit of ideas and techniques. Chapter 9 then looks at the environmental policies that governments manage to deliver in practice.

First we shall review two broad categories of alternative remedies – private actions and government actions.

- Private actions rely entirely on individuals and organizations, unaided by governments, to sort things out. Possibilities here include:

  – Coase bargaining (see Chapter 3)
  – mergers between polluter and pollutee to internalize an externality
  – altruism: increasing green awareness may prompt firms and consumers to produce and buy environmentally friendly products.

- When private actions are inadequate, government intervention may be necessary. This can be a mix of command and control systems and **economic incentive systems.**

Using command and control (CAC) systems the government sets pollution standards or limits. These are enforced by inspection and backed by fines and criminal prosecution for transgression. Such systems simply replace market mechanisms. On the other hand, economic incentive (EI) systems aim to harness and improve, rather than supersede, market forces to achieve environmental ends. The following are some examples of EI systems:

- *Improving existing markets* with 'green' prices, corrected for distorting effects of externalities by means of Pigouvian taxes o subsidies.
- *Creating new markets* by restricting the quantity of pollution, through the issue of a limited number of pollution permits that firms can trade between themselves. This internalizes the pollution externality by putting a price on it. Alternatively, congestion externalities (see Chapter 3), such as on motorways, can be internalized by pricing.
- *Market support* in, for example, the encouragement of the recycling of waste, by means of packaging taxes, recycling credits and disposal charges.

Criteria

How do we decide which of the CAC and EI alternatives is the most effective? Taken from the influential book *Blueprint for a Green Economy,* the quotation which heads this chapter is enthusiastic about the virtues of markets, but in choosing between systems to combat environmental damage the following questions should be considered:

1. Cost

Is pollution being reduced in the most cost-effective manner? Does the anti-pollution strategy give incentives to find better and cheaper ways of achieving environmental quality? Environmental specialists describe this using the acronym **BATNEEC** – *best available technique not entailing excessive cost.*

2. Acceptability

Will the proposed solution command widespread acceptance in the community? This depends partly on whether it is regarded as equitable – not regressive in its income effects, and fair between polluter and pollutee.

The advantages and limitations of CAC and EI systems can be illustrated by comparing a 'green' or pollution tax with direct regulation in the form of an emission standard restricting the amount of pollution. Before we do this we need to make one more comment on variations.

Types of taxes and standards

In the example we shall consider below, it is the quantity of pollution which is taxed – an **emissions** or **effluent tax.** This is the most effective tax because it deals directly with the source of the damage. However, if the measurement of emissions is difficult or costly, then pollution may be taxed indirectly with an **input tax** placed on factors which contribute to the pollution – for example on unleaded petrol or

tilizers. Alternatively, outputs of the polluting manufacturer can be
xed – a **commodity** or **output tax.**

Instead of an emissions standard, the government may enforce a
technology standard, insisting that firms use specific pollution-
reducing equipment (e.g. gas filters on chemical refinery smoke stacks),
or sell products that are designed to minimize pollution costs (e.g. cars
with catalytic converters; aerosols without CFC propellants).

The impact of taxes and standards compared

Figure 11 shows, for a single firm, the marginal social cost of pollution
(MSCP) and the marginal cost of abatement (MCA). If the firm emits
750 units of pollution, an emissions tax of £2 per unit gives a powerful
incentive to abate emissions to 500 units. Between 500 and 750 the
MCA curve lies below the horizontal emissions tax line. Thus the cost
of reducing emissions to 500 units – the shaded area in the diagram – is
less than the tax that would have been paid if emissions had remained
at 750 units. However, the firm has no incentive to reduce pollution
below 500 as the cost of doing so exceeds the emissions tax. The MCA
curve is now *above* the tax line. The least costly option for the firm is to
emit 500 units, paying an emissions tax of £1000 (500 × 2) and to
spend the amount indicated by the shaded area on reducing pollution
from 750 to 500. Thus the tax of £2 induces a socially efficient level of
emissions: at 500 units MCA = MSCP (see Chapter 3 on 'efficient
pollution').

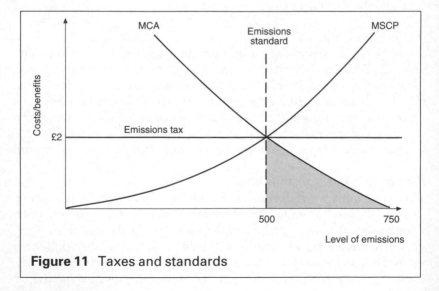

Figure 11 Taxes and standards

Compare this with an **emissions standard** of 500 units, vig
enforced by inspection and fines, which appears to produce exa
same socially efficient outcome. Is there nothing to choose bet
taxes and standards? Pollution taxes, it is claimed, are superio
standards in two respects – costs and incentives.

Costs

Imagine two firms, X and Y, each producing the same level of
emissions, and sufficiently close to each other for the environmental
damage created by each firm's factory chimneys to be the same.
However, if the firms use different production processes, their clean-up
or abatement bills for reducing pollution may differ. It may, for
example, be more costly for firm X to reduce its emissions by 50 per
cent than an equivalent reduction by firm Y.

This is shown in Figure 12, where the marginal cost of abatement
curve for firm X (MCA_X) is above that of firm Y (MAC_Y). For the sake
of clarity, this diagram does not include an MSCP curve as shown in
Figure 11. Assume that it is estimated that the efficient level of
pollution in this case requires total emissions from both firms together
to be no greater than 10 units. As Figure 12 indicates, without any
government intervention, X and Y would each pollute to a level of 10
units, giving a total of 10 + 10 = 20 units.

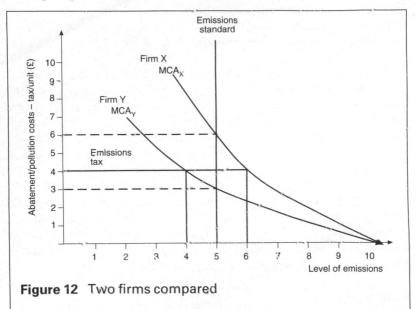

Figure 12 Two firms compared

suppose that the government wishes to reduce the total level of ons from 20 units to the environmentally efficient level of 10 . It decides to achieve this by imposing an emission standard, ricting each firm's emissions to 5 units. This gives the target level of units (5 units (firm X) + 5 units (firm Y)) but it is not the least costly way of reducing total emissions to 10 units. Figure 12 shows why. Recall that the total abatement cost of reducing emissions from one level to another is equal to the corresponding area under the MCA curve. If you are unsure about this, glance back at Figure 11, where the total cost of reducing emissions from 750 to 500 units is the shaded area below the curve. Thus, in Figure 12, the total cost of reducing emissions from 20 to 10 units (a reduction from 10 units to 5 for both X and Y) is firm X's abatement costs – the area under MCA_X between 10 units and 5 units *plus* firm Y's abatement costs – the area under MCA_Y between 10 units and 5 units.

As Figure 12 indicates, setting an emissions standard of 5 units for each firm is an unnecessarily expensive way of reaching the target of 10 units, because it breaks the **equi-marginal rule** for cost minimization. At the margin – reducing emissions from 6 to 5 units – the marginal abatement costs of the two firms should be equal. A comparison of the area in Figure 12 under MCA_X between 5 and 6 units, with the corresponding area under MCA_Y shows that marginal abatement costs for firm X are substantially higher than for firm Y. At the very limit of the marginal unit, as each firm reaches the required emissions standard of 5 units, it can be seen that the marginal abatement cost of X is £6 and that of Y is £3.

If an emissions tax of £4 is introduced in place of a standard, each firm will decide to what extent it is cheaper to reduce emissions and avoid the tax, or to pay the tax. Firm X, with the higher abatement costs, will reduce pollution from 10 to only 6 units but firm Y, with lower abatement costs, from 10 units to 4 units. At this point the marginal abatement costs of both firms are £4 – equal to the tax – conforming to the equi-marginal principle necessary for efficiency. With the emissions tax there is a saving in the total cost of abatement. The £6 marginal cost of abatement from 6 to 5 units for firm X, necessary with a standard, is replaced, under the tax, with a £4 marginal cost reduction by firm Y. Again, if you are unsure about this simply compare, for the emissions standard and the emissions tax, the sum of the total areas under the relevant sections of the MCA curves.

Incentives

With an emissions standard of 5 units, firm X has some incentive to

adopt the superior technology of firm Y, moving to the lo
curve and reducing its costs. However, with the emissions tax
has an even greater incentive to reduce its abatement cost, be
will also reduce its tax liability. *Thus, tax provides a constant sp*
firms to adopt the most efficient abatement technology and so ach
the cleanest possible environment. This is in addition to the advanta
previously noted, of the incentive to reduce costs in accord with th
equi-marginal principle.

Does the polluter really pay?

A pollution tax is popularly thought to be fair because it seems to force
producers, who are mistakenly regarded as the only source of
pollution, to pay the tax – the PPP principle. What about consumers? It
can be argued that they must also share some of the burden because
they buy the goods which ultimately cause the pollution. *In fact, the*
impact of a pollution tax is likely to be divided between producers and
consumers.

Suppose pollution is handled by a *commodity tax* – in the form of a
fixed tax per unit produced. Such a tax will probably see firms attempt
to protect their profits, by charging a higher price and trying to pass the
tax on to consumers (see Figure 13(a)). Although after tax the price
which consumers pay, P_t, is higher than the original price P_0, they do
not pay the full amount of the tax. Some of this is paid by producers,
who now receive P_t minus tax per unit sold – less than the original
price P_0.

Figures 13(a)–(c) show that the division of the pollution tax paid by
producers and consumers depends, *with a given supply curve,* on the
price elasticity of demand. The less price-elastic the demand curve, the
greater the proportion of tax paid by consumers – Figure 13(b). The
more price-elastic the curve, the more will be paid by producers –
Figure 13(a). The incidence of tax is shared equally in Figure 13(c).

Although there will be some welfare losses from the tax – producers
and consumers will buy and sell less than before – the net effect will be
a gain for the community. The excessive pollution damage, previously
unchecked because of externalities, is now at a socially efficient level.
The tax-adjusted green price gives an accurate message to guide producers and consumers. If, for example, the demand for a good causing
pollution is substantially price-elastic, then the green price will
encourage consumers to switch to less damaging alternatives.

Pollution taxes are sometimes denounced because they seem to be
harsh on poor people. The Institute of Fiscal Studies has, for example,
calculated that a 15 per cent tax on domestic fuel in the UK would result

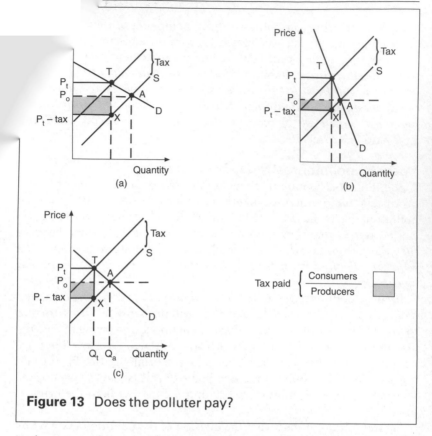

Figure 13 Does the polluter pay?

in the poorest households having to pay more as a proportion of their income (1.8 per cent) than the richest households (0.1 per cent) – an example of a *regressive tax*. However, the regressive effects can be reduced by targeting income supplements and tax concessions to the less well off. Moreover, the revenues from a pollution tax can be used by the government for grants to firms to encourage the development of products and processes that are environmentally less damaging.

Why standards?

We have shown that use of a pollution tax – a market-based system – has in theory considerable advantages over direct regulation of the command and control (CAC) type. Despite this, CAC systems, especially standards, are still the most widely used means of pollution control for the following reasons.

Popularity

- Standards, which appear to promise to reduce pollution to definite *
els, are favoured by politicians and the public. They are simple to u
derstand and have emotional appeal. Even if standards are sometime
inefficient and not always enforced, headlines proclaiming 'tough anti-
pollution legislation' are more likely to win votes than taxes. To de-
clare something illegal gives the impression that action has been taken.

> The reluctance of the UK government, fearing the wrath of motorists, to
> introduce road pricing schemes to ease congestion is a good example of
> the problem of public acceptability. Standards in the form of parking
> zones, speed restrictions and road management are not an efficient
> solution, nor is road building (see Chapter 3 on Congestion) but they are
> more popular with the public than pricing.

- Standards are popular with administrators because less information
is required for the introduction of the standards than with taxes.
They also gain, in preference to taxes, grudging support from industry, especially from large firms who see possibilities for **regulatory
capture** – persuading the pollution regulators to be sympathetic and
'reasonable' when setting and enforcing standards.
- A strong reason for preferring standards is the difficulty in obtain-
ing satisfactory international agreements between governments on
terms of pollution taxes. If pollution tax is imposed by one country
alone it may put its producers at a disadvantage compared with
overseas competitors. If consumers switch to purchasing imports,
the level of pollution may not fall but its source will move abroad.
However, it must be remembered that standards also create costs for
an industry and international agreements on standards are equally
desirable.

Safety thresholds

The vigorous enforcement of clearly defined standards may be the most
suitable way of controlling highly concentrated, life-threatening pollutants – radioactive and certain chemical wastes – where it is essential
that discharges are kept within tightly prescribed limits. In cases of this
kind, safety rather than economy is clearly paramount. Nevertheless, for
the bulk of pollution, the marginal damage curve rises only slowly. *In
such circumstances market-based incentives, rather than standards, will
produce a cleaner environment at lower cost.*

~ets in pollution rights

advantages of market incentive systems can be combined with
.ect regulation by standards (refer back to Figure 12).

Assume, as before, two firms X and Y. The government sets an upper
limit on total daily emissions of 10 units. Accordingly X and Y
are issued with **tradeable pollution permits** (TPPs) allowing each of
them 5 units of emissions. Since X and Y, without restriction, would
each emit 10 units, a 5 unit per day abatement is required from each
firm. The government allows the two firms to trade pollution permits
between themselves for whatever price they can earn.

It will cost firm X, with the higher abatement curve, £6 to reduce
its emissions from 6 units to the 5 units allowed by its permits. It
would therefore gain, if instead of reducing its emissions to 5 units, it
could buy an extra pollution permit for less than £6 allowing it to
pollute up to 6 units. Firm Y, with a lower abatement cost, will find it
profitable to reduce its pollution below 5 units, selling one of its pollution permits for more than £4 – its marginal cost of abatement
from 5 to 4 units. Between £4 and £6, the pollution permits will
be traded. Firm X will now emit 6 units and firm Y will emit 4 units.

Some critics mistakenly regard this exchange as unethical and call
pollution permits *'cancer bonds'*. The market in TPPs has simply
internalized and priced an externality. The target of 10 units has been
achieved with minimum cost – the same effect as an emissions tax.
However, TPPs unite the administrative advantages of standards with
the benefits of market-driven incentives to reduce costs. They may also
be more welcome to industry than taxes. A potential drawback of TPPs
is that they may do nothing to reduce pollution in heavily polluted
areas if the dirty factories (e.g. firm X in Figure 12) are concentrated in
the same region, while clean factories are elsewhere. If there is a lack of
competition among firms wishing to sell permits, they may behave
monopolistically, making permit prices inefficiently high.

Clearly a successful TPP market depends upon the competitiveness
of the market, the way permits are allocated, and the effectiveness of
the agency running the scheme. Despite these rigorous requirements
TPP schemes are gaining international acceptance. The use of trading
permits for carbon dioxide, the principal greenhouse gas, for example,
is growing in Europe, with the UK (see Chapter 9) playing a leading
role.

```
                         KEY WORDS
Economic incentive systems    Technology standard
BATNEEC                       Emissions standard
Emissions/effluent tax        Equi-marginal rule
Input tax                     Regulatory capture
Commodity/output tax          TPPs
```

Further reading

Bamford, C., Chapter 3 in *Transport Economics*, 3rd edition, Heinemann, 2001

Grant, S., and Vidler, C., Section 3.7 in Economics AS for AQA, Heinemann, 2003

Grant, S., and Vidler, C., Section 2.12 in Economics AS for Edexcel, Heinemann, 2003

Munday, S., Chapter 6 in *Markets and Market Failure*, Heinemann, 2000

Useful websites

UK Environmental Protection Agency: www.environment-agency.gov.uk/

DETR: www.roads.detr.gov.uk/itwp/paper/index.htm

Essay topics

1. (a) Explain why the socially optimum level of pollution is not zero. [10 marks]
   (b) Discuss whether taxation or pollution permits is more likely to be effective in reducing pollution to the socially optimum level. [15 marks]
2. (a) Distinguish between private and social benefits. [10 marks]
   (b) Evaluate the policy measures a government could adopt to increase the use of public transport. [15 marks]

Data response question

This task is taken from a question set by the OCR board in 2001. Read the extracts and then answer the questions that follow.

The problem of global warming

The problem of global warming is caused by the emission of 'greenhouse gases', notably carbon dioxide, into the atmosphere. This process appears to be causing climatic changes and rising sea levels.

The effects of global warming can be understood through economic theory. They represent costs that are imposed on one group by the actions of another group. Economists see this as a typical example of market failure that may lead to government intervention.

The following extracts outline some of the issues surrounding global warming.

Extract A

Prescott issues climate warning

Deputy Prime Minister, John Prescott, has insisted that industrialized nations must take urgent action to combat greenhouse gases and climate change. This seems to reflect the views of many scientists who believe that climatic change is being caused by pollution from transport and industry, especially in more wealthy economies. Such views have (5) gained the strong support of developing countries, especially low-lying ones vulnerable to flooding, who see the need for urgent change.

At the World Climate Summit held in Kyoto, Japan, in 1997, many of the main developed nations agreed to cut greenhouse gas emissions by 6% by 2010. Mr Prescott said: 'Time is running out. Developed countries (10) need to start taking action now if they are to meet their Kyoto targets.'

Adapted from *BBC News*, 24 August 2000

Extract B

New energy tax will hit Labour heartlands

Engineering industries in areas of traditional Labour support will suffer most from the Government's new energy tax[1] (the Climate Change Levy), an employers' group claimed yesterday. The levy means that companies are taxed on the amount of energy they use. It has been introduced by the Government to meet targets for the reduction of (5) greenhouse gases. The Engineering Employers' Federation (EEF) has estimated that some companies stand to lose more than £400,000 a year as a result of this tax. The main burden of the tax, which starts in 2001, will fall on companies with large energy bills, particularly large manufacturing and engineering businesses. (10)

The Shadow Chancellor, Michael Portillo, said the cost to businesses of the new energy tax would make British industries less competitive. 'The Government is piling extra costs onto manufacturing businesses at a time when they can least afford it,' said Mr Portillo. 'The environment won't benefit if the energy tax makes British producers lose business to (15) others overseas whose environmental standards are often lower.'

[1] An energy tax is an example of what economists call a 'carbon tax' or, more broadly, a 'green tax'.

Adapted from *The Independent*, 29 August 2000

1. (a) Describe what is meant by the term 'negative exter.
   marks]
   (b) Using Extract A, identify one negative externality that
   arise as a result of global warming. Explain your answer. [4 m.
2. (a) Define what is meant by 'allocative efficiency'. [2 marks]
   (b) Explain why negative externalities prevent allocative efficien
   being achieved. [4 marks]
3. (a) Describe what is meant by an energy tax (Extract B, line 2).
   [2 marks]
   (b) Using a diagram, explain how an energy tax can be used to
   overcome the problem of negative externalities. [10 marks]
4. (a) Extract B refers to some of the limitations of using an energy tax.
   Identify and explain **two** limitations of such a tax. [6 marks]
   (b) Comment upon whether a world tax on energy use would be
   more effective than such a tax imposed by just one country.
   [5 marks]
5. As alternatives to the use of 'green taxes', the UK government could
   consider a range of other policies in order to reduce negative
   externalities. These alternative policies are direct government
   regulation, subsidies to producers and consumers, and marketable
   pollution permits.
   Discuss the likely effectiveness of one of these policies in reducing
   emissions of greenhouse gases. [10 marks]
   [Q1, OCR, Paper 2882, June 2001]

Eight

₁ronmental improvement in theory:
₁vate action

How, from shelves stacked with products labelled "non-toxic", "recycled" and "natural", does the consumer know which to take seriously?'

This chapter looks at the highly pro-market view – *that private action, not involving the government, can solve environmental problems.*

Coase bargaining, private property and mergers

We saw in Chapter 3, with the example of the over-exploitation of fishing fields (Figure 8), how externalities can arise with a common property resource, owned by nobody and to which everyone has free access. As the economist Coase has pointed out, common property resources are likely to be misused and wasted. For instance, it is said that the reason the Indian elephant survives is because it is privately owned, whereas the African elephant, an endangered species threatened by poachers – even in game reserves – is common property.

The Coase argument (point 3 in the boxed summary on the next page) appears to stand on its head the conventional wisdom that the polluter pays. However, the polluter is not always rich and powerful and the pollutee is not always poor and helpless. If polluters are countries that are less well developed, or with inadequate technology and resources, then financial inducements from the 'victim' are essential. Examples of the victim paying the polluter can be seen in the case of technical aid from Sweden to help Poland reduce its emissions of sulphur and nitrogen oxide that cause acid rain, and agreements to transfer technology to China and India to assist with curbing CFC emissions.

Why, according to Coase, is the efficient outcome not affected by who owns property? Imagine a factory whose operations require discharge of some waste into a river, which is also used by a firm running a holiday camp with recreational bathing, boating and fishing. Suppose an efficient solution requires the factory to install filtering equipment to remove unsightly and toxic substances from the effluent,

---

THE COASE THEOREM SUMMARIZED

1. If property ownership is well defined, individuals we informed and bargaining costs not high, then the parties involved can bargain to their mutual benefit.

2. Externalities, positive or negative, will be internalized and included in the negotiated price, allowing a socially efficient output to be achieved.

3. Irrespective of who owns the property rights, a socially efficient outcome can be accomplished even if the pollutee pays the polluter not to pollute.

4. If bargaining is too expensive, it may be possible to seek compensation for pollution damage through the courts.

---

making the river safer and more appealing to holiday-makers. The impact of the filtering plant on the factory and the holiday firm is shown in the first two columns of Table 8.

If the factory owned the river, with a right to discharge waste, the holiday camp would gain if it paid the factory to install a filter. It might, for example, be prepared to pay up to £300 000 – half of its anticipated increase in the profit with a cleaner river – which more than compensates the factory for its fall in profits using the filter. Alternatively, if the holiday camp owned the river, with a right to clean water, then the factory would be compelled to install a filter if it wished to discharge waste. Regardless of property ownership, the same efficient outcome is achieved – filtered river water. The only difference that ownership makes is in the distribution of profits.

A merger of the two firms also solves the problem. Because the increase in total combined profit (the last column in the table) accrues

Table 8 Factory/amenity example

	Factory profits (£)	Holiday camp profits (£)	Merger (£)
No filtering equipment	900	200	1100
Filtering equipment	700	800	1500

FRUIT AND HONEY

ıit-growing and bee-keeping provide a good example of how Coase ıargaining deals with, in this instance, positive externalities. Bees are essential to pollinate fruit blossom, which in turn provides the bees with nectar for honey. The positive externalities arise because extra fruit trees bring extra benefits to bee-keepers for which they do not have to pay. Also, extra beehives bring free benefits to fruit-growers. Theoretically we might expect an under-supply of orchards and bee-hives. However, because property rights in both are well defined, orchard-owners with trees low in nectar yield will pay bee-keepers to place hives in their orchards to achieve effective pollination. Conversely, bee-keepers will pay orchard-owners where there is high nectar-yielding blossom needed for honey.

---

to the merged company, there is a powerful incentive to install a filtering plant. In this case, the diversification by merger internalizes the externality. The firm Ready Mixed Concrete, for example, diversified in this way into the leisure industry. The unsightly water-filled craters – an externality – left by its gravel digging were attractively landscaped and turned into a marina and theme park. However, mergers are usually undertaken to secure economies of scale and finance. They do not offer a general solution for externalities.

Implications and objections

For market enthusiasts, the Coase analysis appears to convey strong pro-market messages:

- If individual property rights are well defined, government action will not be needed. Private bargaining will deal with externalities.
- If common property resources are privatized and run for profit, by charging users for access, then most environmental problems would be solved.

We can identify several objections to the analysis.

1. Inefficient bargaining

Bargaining over externalities may be prohibitively difficult and expensive because thousands of polluters and pollutees are involved. With so many interested parties, free-riders are almost inevitable. Each individual has an incentive to leave others to do the work, but hopes to reap the benefit. Consequently insufficient effort goes into the bargaining.

Frequently information for efficient bargaining is lacking. This is a problem of **asymmetric information** – buyers and sellers have different information about a transaction. The exact sources of pollution may not be known. Moreover, one party may incorrectly believe that it can secure big advantages by tough bargaining. The factory in the example above might demand £600 000 and the negotiations would fail entirely.

In the real world, the ownership of property has a strong impact on bargaining outcomes. Farmers, for example, are a powerful and persuasive political lobby, influencing government legislation within which negotiations about externalities occur.

2. Privatization and externalities

Private ownership of property is clearly irrelevant in the case of a major source of externality – air pollution. It is also unlikely to deal adequately with over-fishing and ocean pollution. Quite apart from the trouble of satisfactorily dividing the world's oceans between countries and transferring ownership to private corporations, there remains the difficulty that fish will swim freely between seas; similarly with the movement of current-borne pollutants. Private ownership alone does not ensure the detection and policing, on an international scale, of the dumping and spillage of pollutants.

The failure of private ownership to deal with externalities arising from cross-boundary problems is also seen in agriculture. Toxic fertilizers used on one farm can percolate through the soil to underground aquifers, contaminating water supplies over a wide area. Likewise, new breeds of pesticide-resistant insects will move freely between farms.

Unless all externalities are internalized and appear in a firm's balance sheet, private ownership of resources provides an incomplete answer. Privatization of forests, for example, might save timber but will not save a single species of plant or animal if such preservation is not profitable. Even reforestation cannot be guaranteed if a logging company has a large enough acreage of timber to last over what it sees as its foreseeable lifetime.

The preservation of endangered species (see the boxed item on the next page) is a further example of how property rights do not get all relevant values on to a balance sheet and included in decisions on the best use of resources. Rhino and elephant farms may succeed in saving the animals, but is this the preferred solution? The 'for profit' answer is regarded by some as a distasteful variant of factory farming. Many people place a higher value on protection of wildlife in its *natural habitat.*

Altruism

If people are sufficiently unselfish (altruistic) and well informed, then in deciding between two almost identical products A and B they will buy B, the more expensive but less environmentally damaging product. In choosing B, consumers are internalizing the externality that exists with A. If there are enough buyers, profitable markets for green products will develop and many environmental problems will be solved.

Increasingly consumers have opportunities to buy environment-friendly products which sell at a premium. For example, they have a choice between free-range and battery eggs. There is no longer just 'timber' – there is wood from sustainable managed forests and wood of dubious origin (sometimes extracted illegally from indigenous native and biological reserves). There is even the possibility of buying green electricity generated from renewable sources like wind, water and methane gas from rubbish. For such electricity customers would be

Rhino and elephant farms 'would save species'

DAVID NICHOLSON LORD

BIG animals such as rhinoceroses and elephants should be 'privatized' to save them from extinction, according to a leading South African wildlife researcher.

Rhinos, for example, should be farmed for their horn, which is widely prized for its medicinal and aesthetic properties and can be harvested without killing the animal.

International measures to curb trade in endangered species and conserve dwindling numbers appear to have failed, Michael Sas-Rolfes told a conference in London yesterday. Both elephant and rhino poaching continued despite millions of pounds spent by government and voluntary bodies.

Mr Sas-Rolfes is preparing a report on the rhino-horn trade for Traffic, a British-based body monitoring trade in endangered species and funded by the World Wide Fund for Nature and the IUCN (World Conservation Union).

He told the conference, organized by the right-wing Institute of Economic Affairs and described as the first in the United Kingdom to propose free-market solutions to environmental problems, that the 'mental block' of Westerners about the commercialization of wild animals could propel many species into extinction.

He argued that the international ban on ivory has only affected Western countries, and demand for rhino horn remained 'substantial' and was unlikely to be reduced. 'As long as there is some demand, rhinos will continue to be under pressure,' he said.

The Independent, 17 April 1994

expected to pay a premium price – possibly 10 per cent more t ordinary bills.

Assuming shoppers can afford green products, there remains the prob lem of **asymmetric information**. Buyers are often less well informed than sellers about the qualities of the products they are buying but also less able to interpret conflicting claims made about them by experts. Witness the controversy over genetically modified (GM) foods. Despite the claim that 25 000 field trials in 45 different countries, involving 60 different species, demonstrate the safety of GM foods, consumers are unconvinced. Fears remain about possible long-term effects on health and the environment. The public need to be reassured not only about

From poachers to gamekeepers

The timber industry is turning over a new leaf. These days, environmentalists are not the only people who are proclaiming the importance of protecting trees. From forestry companies to superstores, those who make their livings cutting them down and selling the resulting wood are also interested in being seen as green and wholesome. And what better way to achieve that image than a certificate issued by a respectable conservation group?

The most respectable of all the groups that certify the ecological soundness of the management of forests is the Forest Stewardship Council (FSC), which is based in Mexico and backed by the World Wide Fund for Nature (more familiarly known as WWF). It was founded five years ago by a coalition of conservation organizations, indigenous people's groups, forest managers and timber companies, and it now has 257 member organizations.

The FSC aims to give wood-buyers a guarantee that their supplies are not harming local people, exploiting their workers, killing rare animals or raping virgin forests in the search for profitable timber.

Although other national and industry schemes also guarantee timber's green credentials, the FSC has the advantage of global standards for accreditation. In Britain, for example, the '95-plus' group of environmentally concerned companies includes firms such as B&Q (a hardware chain), Asda (a supermarket) and Ellis Hill (a timber importer), who want a simple, universal standard to show that their products can be bought with a clear conscience. The FSC provides them with one.

But do shoppers care whether their wood is grown in sustainable forests? Few seem prepared to pay a green premium – B&Q's most optimistic estimate suggests that 15 per cent of its customers might. On the other hand, if all else is equal, shoppers do prefer a store with a responsible image. That gives firms an incentive to improve their green credentials, and hope to trade off the extra cost against a higher turnover.

Source: The Economist Newspaper Limited, London, August 1998

quality of GM testing and licensing but also, as an important first
-p, by clear labelling. This at least gives them the choice of buying
on-genetically modified foods. But is labelling the answer to creating a
market for green products?

*How, from shelves stacked with products labelled 'non-toxic',
'recycled' and 'natural', does the consumer know which to take
seriously?* Which is greener – a product made of bio-degradable
material or of recycled material? Competing claims to greenness may
be confusing for consumers and difficult to evaluate (see the boxed item
on the previous page). Many products are virtuously claimed to be
'green' but how many really are? The label 'recyclable' may mean very
little when there are inadequate facilities to salvage cans and wrappers.
The 'Earth' beer – presented as a breakthrough in environmental
products, with the slogan 'Thinking about the Earth' – offered nothing
more revolutionary than a stay-on can opener.

The consumer may not know if product A (more expensive) is
genuinely environment-friendly, but suspect that the claims are simply
'marketing hype'. The good products will be undercut by the bad and it
will become increasingly difficult to sell genuinely green commodities.
Because of asymmetric information, market forces will not ensure a
socially efficient outcome. A case can be made for some kind of
regulatory body, assessing and validating the claims of eco-labels. *The
Economist's* article 'From poachers to gamekeepers' well illustrates the
importance for consumer confidence of a labelling authority that is
seen to be independent.

Summing up

- Economic analysis shows that government action to deal with environmental problems will usually be more successful if it harnesses
  market forces, instead of replacing them entirely by direct regulation (CAC). Nevertheless, for practical and political reasons, CAC
  systems remain widespread.
- Private action based on property rights (Coase bargaining) or altruism will generate, through market prices, strong but inadequate
  incentives for the best use of environmental resources.
- Market forces alone will not solve environmental problems.
  Government intervention is needed to support and guide private
  action towards a better environment.

```
                            KEY WORDS

    Coase theorem                    Asymmetric information
```

Further reading
Bamford, C., Chapter 5 in *Transport Economics*, 3rd edn, Heinemann, 2001

Bowers, J., Chapter 4 in *Sustainability and Environmental Economics*, Longman, 1999

Grant, S., and Vidler, C., Section 2.11 in Economics AS for Edexcel, Heinemann, 2003

Perman, R., Common, M., McGilvray, J. and Ma, Y., Chapters 7 and 8 in *Natural Resources and Environmental Economics*, Longman, 1999.

Useful websites
DETR: www.roads.detr.gov.uk/roadnetwork/heta/hetacoba.htm
Severn–Trent: www.severn-trent.com/

Essay topics
1. (a) Explain the Coase theorem. [10 marks]
   (b) Discuss how useful the Coase theorem is. [15 marks]
2. (a) Distinguish between a public good, a private good and a quasi public good. [10 marks]
   (b) Discuss what type of good the environment is. [15 marks]

Data response question
This task is based on a question set by Edexcel in 2002. Study the information and then answer the questions that follow.

Extract A

Paying for congestion

No one doubts that Britain's transport system is in a mess. Increased incomes and car ownership have meant that road traffic has grown by more than 70% in the past 20 years. Under-investment has left local roads in their worst condition for 30 years. Public transport fails to offer an adequate alternative and its use has declined. Chronic congestion has (3) been the inevitable result — damaging economic prospects, the quality of life, public safety, and the environment.

The long-term solution to the congestion problem is to increase the cost of driving on congested roads. Road space is a scarce resource and motorists should pay more to reduce congestion. It is estimated that (1C urban road charges in peak hours, and motorway and trunk road tolls, charged only in busy hours, would reduce total congestion by a quarter.

Source: adapted from *The Financial Times*, 21 July 2000

Extract B

Toll tax

Ministers are planning to cut petrol tax by raising billions of pounds from motorway tolls. Gordon Brown, the Chancellor, is preparing to change the way that motorists are taxed after widespread anger at British fuel prices, the highest in Europe.

Mr Brown now believes that motorway tolls will be far more effective (. than fuel prices in reducing congestion on Britain's busiest motorways. He wants to tax congestion rather than rely on a fuel tax that hits millions of motorists, especially from rural areas, who never drive in congested cities or on motorways.

Mr Brown has been told, that by using motorway tolls to replace a (1 proportion of fuel tax, at least 7p a litre could be cut from pump prices.

Treasury officials have been studying the French motorway toll system, which raises about £3 billion a year although it is used less than the British network. Money raised from tolls has led to a huge expansion and improvement of French motorways, among Europe's most efficient. (1

Similar charges of about 6p a mile would raise at least £4 billion in Britain. For example, a motorist driving from Leicester to London on the M1 would pay £6. Whitehall officials argue that a British toll system could be more sophisticated than the French version, with charges varying according to the time of day, possibly with toll-free travel overnight to (2 encourage a more even spread of traffic.

Source: adapted from *The Times*, London, 19 June 2000

Figure A: Percentage of total distance travelled by all mo transport in Great Britain 1958–1998

Year	Buses and coaches	Cars, vans and taxis	Rail	Other
1958	31	44	16	9
1968	16	72	9	3
1978	12	78	7	3
1988	7	84	6	3
1998	6	86	6	2

Figure B: United Kingdom environmental taxes 1995–1999 (£ million, current prices)

	1995	1997	1999
Energy			
Duty on hydrocarbon oil*	15,116	18,058	22,375
VAT on duty	2,645	3,160	3,916
Fossil fuel levy	1,306	418	104
Road vehicles			
Vehicle excise duty	3,954	4,334	4,873
Other environmental taxes **	339	820	1,323
Total environmental taxes	23,360	26,790	32,591
Environmental taxes as % of:			
Total taxes and social contributions	9.2	9.3	9.8
Gross Domestic Product	3.3	3.6	3.7

*Duty on unleaded petrol, leaded petrol, diesel, ultra low sulphur diesel

**Air passenger duty and landfill tax

Source of Figures A and B: ONS Dataset

1. (a) With reference to Figure A, describe the changing patterns in modes of transport in Great Britain over the period shown. [2 marks]
   (b) How would you account for the changing patterns you have described? [6 marks]
2. With reference to Extract A, identify two examples of an external cost, justifying your choice. [4 marks]
3. (a) Explain why road space is considered to be 'a scarce resource' (Extract A, line 9). [2 marks]

Examine the view that in inner cities motorists should pay 'ban road charges in peak hours' (Extract A, line 11). [8 marks]
iscuss why, despite being 'the highest in Europe', fuel taxes have not prevented road congestion in Britain (Extract B, line 4). [6 marks]

5. 'Mr Brown now believes that motorway tolls will be far more effective than fuel prices in reducing congestion on Britain's busiest motorways' (Extract B, lines 5–6).

(a) Illustrating your answer with an appropriate diagram, explain how motorway tolls might reduce road congestion. [6 marks]

(b) Examine two disadvantages of using motorway tolls to control road congestion. [6 marks]

[Q1, Edexcel, Unit 2, January 2002]

Chapter Nine

Environmental improvement in practice

*'Another major priority for economists working in the area of environmental protection is the promotion, where appropriate, of economic instruments, including "**green taxes**", permit trading schemes and liability regimes, as promising ways of tackling environmental problems.'*
Department of Environment, Food and Rural Affairs, 2003

Much of the environmental legislation currently in force in the UK was formulated by the European Commission in Brussels. There have been some British initiatives, however, which are worth noting and they fall into two categories – the regulatory approach and the economic instruments approach. Both approaches are different ways of responding to environmental problems and in practice the government uses a combination of the two as the following summary shows.

Integrated pollution control
The core of UK policy is set out in the Environmental Protection Act 1990, a key element of which is **integrated pollution control** (IPC). Before IPC was established, the releases of polluting substances from industry were regulated separately according to the environmental medium they were released into. The Fifth Report of the Royal Commission on Environmental Pollution published in 1976 argued that this arrangement was unsatisfactory and proposed that one body should regulate the release of prescribed substances. This integrated approach was embedded in the 1990 Act which now requires that an overall assessment be made of the impact of releases into the environment as a whole.

Regulation
Two authorities established in 1996 are responsible for pollution control in the UK – the Scottish Environment Protection Agency and the Environment Agency in England and Wales.
The main features of IPC are:

- It monitors some 2000 processes in all the major industries.
- Those responsible for a polluting process have to apply for prior authorization from the Environment Agency to operate the process.

IPC requires operators to consider the total impact of all releases to air, water and land when making an application.

- The operator has to advertise that an application has been made. Details of this are held in a public register which is available for public inspection. The Environment Protection Act only allows for exclusion of the application from the public register on grounds of commercial confidentiality or National Security. Commercial confidentiality applies only if the operator can prove that release of the information would damage a commercial advantage or produce an unreasonably commercial disadvantage. After four years the information is placed on a public register unless it is determined that it is still commercially confidential.

- After due consideration, the Environment Agency may either approve or reject the application. When granting approval the Environment Agency must ensure that the best available techniques not entailing excessive cost (**BATNEEC**) are used. In addition, if a process involves releases to more than one environmental medium, the operator must use the best practicable environmental option (**BPEO**) to achieve the best overall environmental solution.

- Operators have to monitor their emissions and report them to the Environment Agency on an annual basis.

- If the Environment Agency believes that the operator is breaching the terms of the authorization it can serve an enforcement or prohibition notice.

On 21 March 2003 the organizers of Glastonbury Festival were ordered to pay £13,500 in fines and costs for polluting the river Whitelake that runs through the site of the world famous festival. The case was brought by the Environment Agency whose officers detected high concentrations of ammonia in the river as far as two miles downstream of the Worthy Farm site. Through detailed investigations the problems were traced back to toilet facilities at the festival site. These were found to be leaking and allowing large volumes of sewage to enter the river.

During last year's Festival weekend around 120 fish were found dead in the river Whitelake. Pollution of the water course also occurred as a result of previous festivals and the organizers had received a formal caution after the previous event in 2000. (The Glastonbury Festival was not held in 2001 because of the foot and mouth epidemic.)

Source: Environment Agency

Typically, regulation involves the setting of emission targets for firms and two alternative **regulatory approaches** have evolved – technology-based and performance-based. Technology standards specify the methods and equipment that companies have to use to meet the target. Performance standards set an overall target for each firm or plant but allow them some discretion in how they meet the standards but this ignores the possibility that some operators might be able to make reductions more readily than others.

Regulation

An example of good regulation is the EU National Emissions Ceiling Directive which sets binding targets for the main emissions affecting air pollution, but provides Member States with flexibility about the means to deliver them. The Directive is based on robust science and proper assessment of costs and benefits. It addresses the problem at the right level given that the transboundary nature of some of the pollutants is at the EU level, and it takes account of non-EU countries. It reflects Member States' different situations and different costs and does not seek a 'one size fits all' approach.

Another example of good regulation is the **Montreal Protocol** which aimed to phase out all the main ozone depleting chemicals. The cost of not taking action was high (potential damage to crops and skin cancer for people and animals); there was international agreement to act; business was given a clear signal of the need for action, and regulations in all major industrialized countries ensured that there were no free riders. The Montreal Protocol was implemented in the UK through regulations, resulting in a complete phasing out of production and consumption between 1994 and 1996, at relatively low cost to industry.

The Building Regulations requirements for energy efficiency in new and refurbished buildings are an example of regulations which are set within the UK. Revisions to the regulations are made following a comprehensive evaluation of the costs and benefits. The latest amendments to the regulations for England and Wales took effect from April 2002 and are expected to yield significant benefits in terms of lower heating bills, which may be cut by up to 25 per cent in the case of new dwellings.

An example of poor regulation is the EU Directives on bathing waters. These are based on poor science, are out of date, and do not take proper account of public health effects. The cost of action is disproportionate to the benefits, while the benefits were not properly established before targets were set. The regulations are driven at EU level even though the benefits only apply to those who choose to bathe in UK waters. And the standards are unnecessarily uniform; there is no reason in principle why little-used beaches should need to have the same standards as others with much greater levels of usage.

Source: HM Treasury, *Tax and the Environment: using economic instruments*, November 2002

Although the regulatory approach generally succeeded in reducing emissions from previously unregulated industries, now, more than two decades after their introduction, they are regarded as inefficient, costly and burdensome.

Economic instruments

Economists have long advocated the use of **economic instruments** as alternatives or supplements to regulation. They work by putting a price on the use of the environment and can include taxes, charges, **tradeable permits**, subsidies or tax credits, and deposit/refund schemes. Their major advantage is that they achieve the same level of environmental protection for a lower overall cost. Given the importance of the overall costs of environmental protection in political debate, this is a crucial advantage.

Economic instruments also allow for a more hands-off regulation and decentralized decision-making, giving greater freedom to firms and plants about how to comply.

The UK government recognized these benefits and set out its aims to use the tax system to achieve environmental improvements in its *Statement of Intent on Environmental Taxation* published in 1997. Its achievements were reviewed in 2002 in the Treasury document *Tax and the environment: using economic instruments*. The following section summarizes the progress made with a range of economic instruments.

Climate change levy

At the Earth Summit in Rio in 1992 the developed countries agreed a voluntary target to reduce greenhouse gas emissions to 1990 levels by 2000. Ten years later, in March 2002, the Environment Secretary, Margaret Beckett, was able to announce that the UK was one of the few developed countries to meet this target. At **Kyoto** in 1997, the developed countries agreed a legally-binding commitment to reduce greenhouse gas emissions by 5.2 per cent below 1990 levels over the period 2008–2012. The EU agreed to an 8 per cent reduction. The UK's contribution to this target has been set at a $12\frac{1}{2}$ per cent reduction on 1990 levels in emissions of a basket of six greenhouse gases. The UK has also set itself a domestic objective that goes beyond our legally-binding Kyoto target – to reduce emissions of carbon dioxide by 20 per cent on 1990 levels by 2010. To meet these commitments the government introduced the climate change levy in 2001. It is a tax on electricity, gas, coal and liquefied petroleum gas used by the non-domestic sector and is designed to encourage business to use energy

---

Application of the Climate Change Levy

The levy, introduced on 1 April 2001, was announced in the March 1999 Budget to give businesses a full two years to adjust. Rates of levy are 0.15p/kWh for gas, 1.17p/kg (equivalent to 0.15p/kWh) for coal, 0.96p/kg (equivalent to 0.07p/kWh) for liquefied petroleum gas (LPG), and 0.43p/kWh for electricity. The levy is expected to raise around £1 billion in its first full year (2001/02). The levy package is expected to lead to reductions in carbon dioxide emissions of at least 2.5 million tonnes of carbon a year by 2010.

Source: Defra

---

more efficiently. In order to protect the competitiveness of British firms, the government returns the revenues from the levy to the non-domestic sector, principally through a cut in the rate of employers' National Insurance Contributions of 0.3 percentage points.

Renewables obligation

Introduced in 2001 this imposes a legally enforceable quota on all utility companies to supply electricity from renewable sources such as wind power and solar power. It replaces an earlier system based on individual projects. The government's target is for 10 per cent of all electricity to be generated from renewable sources by 2010. However, Friends of the Earth and the House of Commons Environment Select Committee have both called for this target to be doubled to 20 per cent. Once electricity is generated by a qualifying scheme it can be sold into the electricity market with a **Renewable Obligation Certificate** (ROC). ROCs are tradable which allows electricity suppliers to meet their renewable obligation at minimum cost. Similar schemes are being considered by the Environment Agency for emissions of nitrogen and sulphur dioxides.

Emissions trading scheme

In 2002 the UK government launched the world's first economy-wide greenhouse gas emissions trading scheme which participants can join by bidding for permits, by signing one of the negotiated sectoral agreements, or by developing approved carbon-saving projects. The scheme, which encourages the adoption of the cheapest means of making emissions reductions, has given the UK a head start in emissions trading and will enable the City of London to be an international centre for such trading.

...gates levy

...wing the failure of industry attempts to promote voluntary ...gements, the aggregates levy was introduced in 2002. It is an ...ironmental tax on the commercial exploitation of aggregates in the ...K. The primary objectives of the levy are to reduce the demand for virgin aggregate and encourage the use of alternative materials. Its purpose is to address by taxation the environmental costs associated with quarrying operations, such as noise, dust, visual intrusion, loss of amenity and damage to biodiversity, in line with the government's policy on environmental taxation. The levy was set at a rate of £1.60 per tonne and was accompanied by a 0.1 percentage cut in employers' national insurance contributions.

Landfill tax

This was launched in 1996 to help the government meet the EU Landfill Directive of 1999 which stipulates that by 2013 the UK should reduce biodegradable municipal waste to 50 per cent of that produced in 1995. Currently 78 per cent or 22.1m tonnes of municipal waste out of 28.2m tonnes goes to landfill. Britain's total waste is growing at 3 per cent a year and is expected to double by 2020. The tax is paid on every tonne of waste taken to any of the 2264 landfill sites in the UK. It is paid by the operator of the site but passed on to customers. The standard rate of tax was initially set at £7 per tonne but increased to £10 per tonne in 1999 when the government announced that it would increase by £1 per year until 2004. It is currently £14 per tonne, but in his budget statement in April 2003, the Chancellor announced that it would increase to £15 in 2004. Thereafter the rate will increase by £3 per annum until it reaches the long term goal of £35 per tonne.

Generally speaking market solutions to waste disposal are ineffective because of the externalities involved, as the following section makes clear.

The position on the extreme left of Figure 14 represents a situation in which all waste is landfilled, while on the extreme right all waste is recycled. Moving from left to right, as recycling increases, the marginal cost of recycling (MC_R) rises because of additional costs mainly associated with transportation over greater distance. Similarly, moving from right to left as landfill increases, the marginal social cost of landfill (MSC_l) will also rise.

It can be seen from the lower curve that the marginal private cost of landfill (MPC_L) is less than the marginal social cost of landfill (MSC_L).

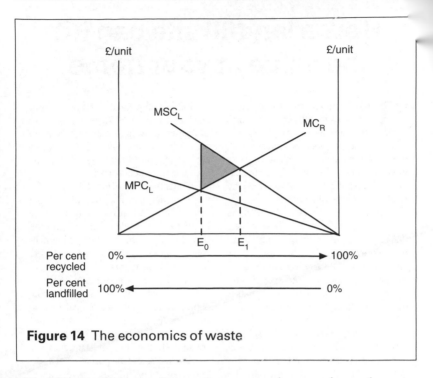

Figure 14 The economics of waste

This difference between the two curves exists because the market price for landfill does not reflect the following externalities:

- loss of land for amenity
- contamination of groundwater by leachate
- emission of methane – a greenhouse gas
- visual disamenity, noise and smells.

The MSC_L curve includes all these costs, however, so the efficient balance between recycling and landfill is at point E_1 where $MSC_L = MC_R$ (the equi-marginal principle). At this point, the total cost to society of waste management would be minimized but because decisions are based on private costs where $MPC_L = MC_R$ not enough recycling occurs and too much waste (E_0) is sent to landfill. The resulting cost burden on society is shown by the shaded area.

Although the landfill tax is theoretically sound it has encountered problems. According to Defra's *Review of the UK Landfill Tax* it has not encouraged people to recycle or compost and 25 per cent of local authorities will fail to meet their recycling targets by 2005/2006.

How a landfill site can hit the value of your home

Two hundred thousand homes close to landfill sites are worth an average £5,500 less because of the nuisance caused by dust, noise, smell and vermin, according to a government report. The value of the nation's housing stock was reduced by £2.48bn because of landfill.

In the first comprehensive look at the effect of landfill sites on house prices, the survey found that in the country as a whole prices were 7 per cent lower near landfill sites. But there were marked regional variations, with the Scots losing 41 per cent of the value of their homes if there was a landfill site within a quarter of a mile.

The survey looked at the sale of 592,000 houses over 10 years, and compared prices of similar properties near the 11,300 landfill sites in the country. Houses within a quarter of a mile of a site were worth on average £5,500 less and those between quarter and half a mile £1,600 less. The purpose of the survey was to help the Treasury measure the loss of amenity value caused by landfill so the landfill tax could be fixed accordingly.

Friends of the Earth said the environment agency had revealed that 56 per cent of the 2,264 current landfill sites in England and Wales were failing to comply with waste management licence conditions, and 14 per cent were 'nowhere near compliance'. FoE's senior waste campaigner, Claire Wilton, said: 'It is perfectly understandable that people do not want to live near landfill sites. Most fail to comply with licence conditions. They are smelly, noisy and create pollution. The government must do more to protect the public from poorly managed landfills and set tough targets to reduce the amount of hazardous waste that is landfilled.'

The Guardian, 22 February 2003

A mixture of policy approaches

Although they are now much more widely used in the UK economic instruments are seldom used alone and are typically supported by a combination of statutory controls, information, government advice and persuasion.

An example of the efficacy of statutory control is shown by provisional figures for 2002, which show continued improvement in urban air quality in England since 1993 because of stringent emission standards. There were 14 days of moderate or higher air pollution on average per urban site in 2002 compared with 59 days in 1993. Under the Air Quality Strategy new targets have been set to cut even further levels of four key air pollutants in England. In respect of particles, the new targets are: